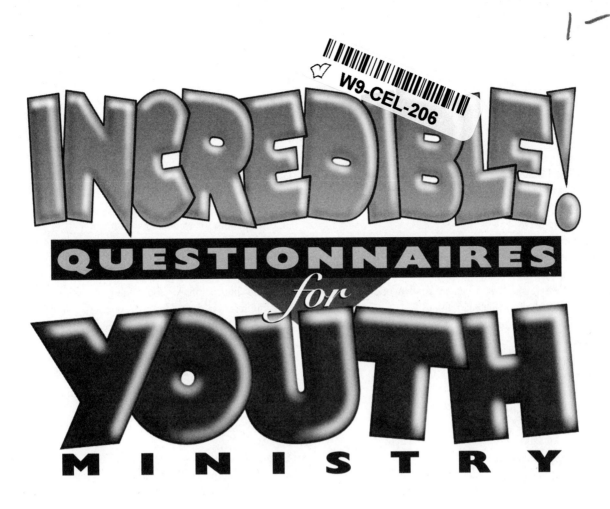

Youth Specialties Titles

Professional Resources
Compassionate Kids
Developing Spiritual Growth in Junior High Students
Equipped to Serve
Help! I'm a Volunteer Youth Worker!
Help! I'm a Sunday School Teacher!
How to Expand Your Youth Ministry
How to Recruit and Train Volunteer Youth Workers
Junior High Ministry (Revised Edition)
The Ministry of Nurture
One Kid at a Time
Peer Counseling in Youth Groups
Advanced Peer Counseling in Youth Groups

Discussion Starter Resources
Get 'Em Talking
High School TalkSheets
Junior High TalkSheets
High School TalkSheets: Psalms and Proverbs
Junior High TalkSheets: Psalms and Proverbs
More High School TalkSheets
More Junior High TalkSheets
Parent Ministry TalkSheets
What If . . . ?
Would You Rather . . . ?

Ideas Library
Ideas Combo 1-4, 5-8, 9-12, 13-16, 17-20, 21-24, 25-28,
    29-32, 33-36, 37-40, 41-44, 45-48, 49-52, 53, 54, 55
Ideas Index

Youth Ministry Programming
Compassionate Kids
Creative Bible Lessons in John: Encounters with Jesus
Creative Bible Lessons on the Life of Christ
Creative Programming Ideas for Junior High Ministry
Creative Socials and Special Events
Dramatic Pauses
Facing Your Future
Great Fundraising Ideas for Youth Groups
Great Ideas for Small Youth Groups

Great Retreats for Youth Groups
Greatest Skits on Earth
Greatest Skits on Earth, Volume 2
Hot Illustrations for Youth Talks
Hot Talks
Junior High Game Nights
More Junior High Game Nights
More Hot Illustrations for Youth Talks
Play It! Great Games for Groups
Play It Again! More Great Games for Groups
Road Trip
Super Sketches for Youth Ministry
Teaching the Bible Creatively
Up Close and Personal: How to Build Community in Your
    Youth Group

Clip Art
ArtSource Volume 1—Fantastic Activities
ArtSource Volume 2—Borders, Symbols, Holidays, and
    Attention Getters
ArtSource Volume 3—Sports
ArtSource Volume 4—Phrases and Verses
ArtSource Volume 5—Amazing Oddities and Appalling Images
ArtSource Volume 6—Spiritual Topics
ArtSource Volume 7—Variety Pack

Video
Edge TV
The Heart of Youth Ministry: A Morning with Mike Yaconelli
Next Time I Fall in Love Video Curriculum
Promo Spots for Junior High Game Nights
Resource Seminar Video Series
Understanding Your Teenager Video Curriculum

Student Books
Grow for It Journal
Grow for It Journal through the Scriptures
Next Time I Fall in Love
101 Things to Do During a Dull Sermon
Wild Truth Journal for Junior Highers

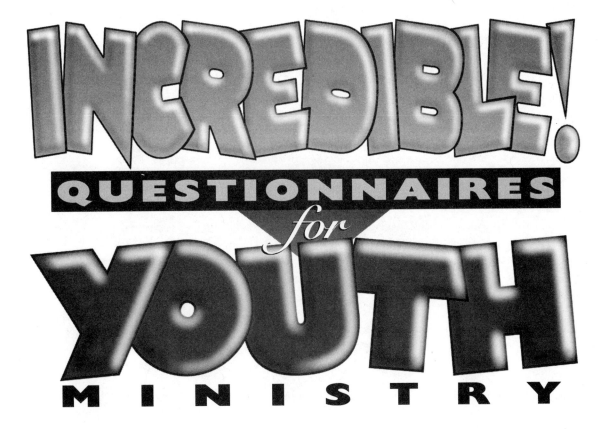

INCREDIBLE!
QUESTIONNAIRES *for* YOUTH MINISTRY

Rick Bundschuh & E.G. Von Trutzschler

Youth Specialties

ZondervanPublishingHouse
Grand Rapids, Michigan

A Division of HarperCollinsPublishers

Incredible Questionnaires for Youth Ministry: 50 ways to find out all sorts of neat stuff about your kids

Copyright © 1995 by Youth Specialties, Inc.

Youth Specialties Books, 1224 Greenfield Drive, El Cajon, California 92021, are published by Zondervan Publishing House, 5300 Patterson, S.E., Grand Rapids, Michigan 49530.

Bundschuh, Rick, 1951-
    Incredible questionnaires for youth ministry: 50 ways to find out all sorts of neat stuff about your kids / Rick Bunschuh and E.G. Von Trutzschler.
      p. cm.
    ISBN 0-310-20770-3 (pbk.)
    1. Church work with teenagers — United States.
  2. Questionnaires — United States. I. Von Trutzschler, E.G.
  II. Title.
 BV 4447.B77 1995
 295'.23 — dc20   95-44534
                                           CIP

Edited by Noel Becchetti and Vicki Newby
Typography and Design by PAZ Design Group

Printed in the United States of America

95 96 97 98 99/ /5 4 3 2 1

Table of Contents

Intoducing
INCREDIBLE!
QUESTIONNAIRES

Kids love to tell you about themselves. **Incredible Questionnaires** is a tool that helps young people do just that—while gaining valuable insight and having fun in the process. You will gain a treasure chest of information about your students as well as opportunities for discussions, teaching, and counseling.

There are fifty questionnaires here, each with a clear set of leader's instructions to help you mine the most value from each questionnaire.

The questionnaires deal with issues relevant to the kids you work with and love. Some are more appropriate for younger students, some for older teens, some are best used with kids who have little Christian background, and some are just right for kids who have been in church so long that they think they know it all. Some can be used to help kids evaluate their own attitudes, ideas, or actions; others can give you profiles of your group in order to be better equipped to understand and serve them. Some are quizzes; others can be used during a particular season or just for fun and games.

The leader guides give you all the information, tips, and steps that you'll need to know to have a winning experience each time.

Together, the questionnaires and leader guides are your key to unlock your students' deepest personal thoughts. Incredible!

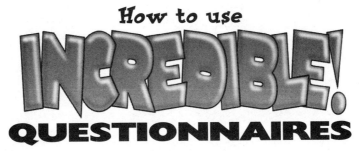

How to use INCREDIBLE! QUESTIONNAIRES

How do you go from your first look at a questionnaire to a successful class experience? Here are some tips:

❶ To pick which questionnaires are best for your situation, ask questions like these: Is the topic hot with my students? Will the students' answers provide me with information I can use? Is there a questionnaire that amplifies a particular Bible study I have in mind?

❷ Once you've picked a questionnaire, check the leader guide information on the back for special instructions. The information will give you important insights into the questions your students will be asked. Spend the time it takes to understand the significance of the questions and possible answers. You'll also find important classroom tips.

❸ Slap your questionnaire on a photocopy machine and make as many copies as you require.

❹ When using a questionnaire, provide a place with enough room, comfortable writing surfaces, and pens or pencils.

❺ Introduce the questionnaire to your kids. This gives you an opportunity to create a nonthreatening atmosphere (this isn't a test, you won't be graded, no one will know who you are, and so forth).

❻ Have your students work privately on these questionnaires. Keep a sharp eye out to ensure that each individual's privacy is respected.

❼ When the questionnaires are completed, collect the papers and pencils and read them over as soon as possible. Evaluate your results, then respond accordingly.

Hints for Success

◆ Use these questionnaires as "seasoning" in your program. Unleashing a steady barrage of questionnaires will decrease the benefits.

◆ Use these questionnaires to discover where your kids lack understanding in their faith. Then present Bible studies and lessons that fill those gaps with God's wisdom.

◆ Use these questionnaires to jump-start a meeting or to get a discussion going.

◆ Use these questionnaires to get an honest reading of the temperature of your group. Don't be surprised if some kids clown around with, or supply shocking information on, their questionnaires.

◆ Most importantly, **do something** with the information you have gleaned. If your group tells you they didn't like the food at camp, change it. If you find an appalling lack of wisdom, education, or insight in your kids, change it!

That's Entertainment!

1. How often do you go to the movies? (check one)
   ___ Two or more times a week
   ___ Once or twice a week
   ___ Once every couple of weeks
   ___ Once a month
   ___ Once every couple of months
   ___ Once or twice a year
   ___ Never

2. How often do you rent or watch videos? (check one)
   ___ Two or more times a week
   ___ Once or twice a week
   ___ Once or twice a month
   ___ Once a month
   ___ Once or twice a year
   ___ Never

3. Do you watch R-rated movies or videos?
   ___ Yes ___ No ___ Depends on the content

4. Do you watch X-rated movies or videos?
   ___ Yes ___ No

5. If you have cable TV or a satellite dish, does your family subscribe to HBO, Showtime, or other pay movie channels?
   ___ Yes ___ No

6. What channel do you watch more than any others (CNN, ESPN, MTV, PBS, CBS, etc.)?

7. Is the TV on most of the time in your home?
   ___ Yes ___ No

8. Do you have your own TV?
   ___ Yes ___ No

9. Do you watch certain TV programs on a regular basis?
   ___ Yes ___ No
   If so, which one(s)?

10. Do you record programs that you want to watch later?
    ___ Often ___ Sometimes ___ Never

11. How many hours do you spend watching TV each week? (circle one)
    0-1   2-4   5-9   10-15
    16-20   21-25   26-30   Over 30

12. Are programs or videos that contain swear words watched in your home?
    ___ Yes ___ No

13. In your opinion, what are the three best television programs on the air? Which are the three worst?

    Best   Worst

    1._____   1._____

    2._____   2._____

    3._____   3._____

14. What three movies are most popular with you and your friends right now?

    1.

    2.

    3.

15. Who are the three actors and actresses most popular with you and your friends right now?

    Actresses   Actors

    1.   1.

    2.   2.

    3.   3.

HOW TO USE
That's Entertainment!

This questionnaire helps you see the influences your students are allowing into their lives. You can see how much time your students spend being entertained (or possibly poisoned) by movies and television. You can get an idea of which films or film stars are influencing your kids and what your kids are watching on TV. Also, if there is a movie or TV program that is the rage among your kids, this questionnaire will bring it to the surface. It may be a good idea to watch that movie or program yourself so you know what it is saying to your students.

A number of Bible studies or lessons can spin off from this information. Contrast the values presented by particular films and videos with those that our Lord taught. Talk about how students can become discerning and able to separate the good from the garbage. Go over the importance of making the most of one's time.

Suggested classroom activities

To kick off discussion, show part or all of a popular video. Better still, assemble a video that features clips from many programs. One or two of your kids could do this in advance.

Thinking through the questions

The questions cover three main issues. There is the issue of propriety ("garbage in, garbage out") — questions 3, 4, and 12. The issue of time is raised in questions 1, 2, 7, and 9-11. Questions 13-15 will give you insight into your students' tastes and values.

ROCKS in my Head

1. Which type of music do you most like to listen to?
   (circle all that apply)

Oldies	Techno	Hip hop
Country	Rave	Dance
Reggae	Big band	Elevator music
Classical	Folk	Punk
Vintage rock	Folk rock	Gospel
Alternative rock	Lounge music	Metal
Jazz	Worship	Rap
Top 40	Blues	Opera
Easy Listening		

2. How do you get most of your music? (check one)
   ___ With my own money
   ___ Gifts from others
   ___ Tape it from the collections of others

3. How many hours a day do you listen to music? (circle one)
   0-1   2-3   4-7   More than 7

4. Who are your top five favorite bands or performers?

   1.

   2.

   3.

   4.

   5.

5. How often do you attend concerts? (circle one)
   Never   Seldom   Sometimes   Often

6. Could you go for two weeks without listening to any
   music? (circle one)
   Sure   Probably   Probably not

7. How much money do you think you spend monthly on
   music? (circle one)
   $15 $20 $30 $40   Over $40

8. Do you and your parents have disagreements over the kind
   of music that you listen to?
   ___ Yes ___ No ___ Sometimes

9. Do you think some kinds of music should be kept from
   being played on the radio?
   ___ Yes ___ No
   Why or why not?

10. Is there any music or musical groups that you think a
    Christian should not listen to?
    ___ Yes ___ No
    Why or why not?

    If yes, what music or musical groups?

11. What percentage of music you listen to is Christian
    music? (circle the correct percentage)
    0 5 10 20 30 40 50 60 70 80 90 100

12. Do you think the music coming out of the Christian
    community usually competes favorably with secular music?
    ___ Yes ___ No ___ Don't know

13. Do you have tapes or CDs that you would not want your
    parents or minister to hear you listening to?
    ___ Yes ___ No

14. Do you own any music with swear words, dirty themes,
    or explicit sexual content?
    ___ Yes ___ No

15. Do you think music affects a person's mood?
    ___ Yes ___ No

16. Do you think music can affect a person's behavior
    or lifestyle?
    ___ Yes ___ No

HOW TO USE
Rocks in my Head

This questionnaire is designed to help you discover what your kids are listening to, how they think and feel about music, and how much of their time and money is being invested in their music.

Musical tastes vary widely with age and maturity. A junior high student will usually have significantly different answers than a high school student.

Caution must be used not to take the answers that kids give and use them as excuses to "beat up the troops" with anti-music ragings and "thou shalt not" diatribes. Instead, use the answers and the dilemmas posed by them to allow the kids to wrestle through the issues and to come to conclusions and solutions themselves.

Bible studies built upon this questionnaire can include a look at music in the Bible, worship, and a comparison of godly and worldly values.

Suggested classroom activities

Show a popular music video or play a recording while you display the lyrics. Interesting discussions can be built on these lyrics.

Thinking through the questions

Questions 1-7 deal primarily with musical tastes and the amount of time and energy a person devotes to music. Use this information to your advantage. For example, if concert going is big with your kids (question 6), encourage some students to form a band or schedule a group outing to a Christian concert this year.

Questions 8-14 deal with the positive and negative influences of music. You will learn how much of each your students tend to hear.

Questions 15 and 16 can lead to an interesting controversy and a discussion of how external influences shape our personal attitudes and actions and those of our society.

CLOTHES HORSE

Age _____ Male _____ Female _____ Grade _____ School _____

1. What kind of clothes are popular with the guys in your school right now?

2. What kind of clothes are popular with the girls in your school right now?

3. Are there any kinds of apparel that are not permitted at your school?
   ___ Yes ___ No
   If, so what?

4. Do you agree with school bans on clothing?
   ___ Yes ___ No
   Why or why not?

5. Do you think people judge others by the clothes they wear?
   ___ Yes ___ No

6. How important to you are the clothes you wear? (circle one)
   Extremely   Very   Somewhat
   Sort of   Not important at all

7. Do you dress the way that you do to make a "statement" or identify with any particular group or lifestyle?
   ___ Yes ___ No
   If yes, which?

8. What kind of "look" do you think is out or lame? Why?

9. What are some of the new fashion trends you see emerging?

10. Would you tell a friend your honest opinion if he or she wore something that you thought was ugly or unstylish?
    ___ Yes ___ No

11. Do you think people should dress up to go to church?
    ___ Yes ___ No
    Why or why not?

12. How much do you spend on clothes in a month? (circle one)
    $10 or less $20 $50 $75 $100 or more

13. Do you think that modesty is something that should be considered when selecting clothing?
    ___ Yes ___ No
    How would you define modesty?

14. Would you say something to a friend if you thought his or her clothes were immodest?
    ___ Yes ___ No

15. Is there any kind of clothing that parents forbid you to wear?
    ___ Yes ___ No
    If yes, what is it?

16. Do you have regular arguments in your home about clothing?
    ___ Yes ___ No

17. Do you think parents should have a say in what their kids wear?
    ___ Yes ___ No
    Why or why not?

HOW TO USE
Clothes Horse

Clothes are a big part of the lives of most teens. Clothing defines what "tribe" the student identifies with, and there are often perceived status levels or personal statements woven into the fabric.

This questionnaire can be used for a number of purposes. You can gather interesting information about your group's attitudes regarding clothing and style. You can see how "into" fashion and style the girls or guys in your group are. You can gather information about imminent fashion trends that can be used in a variety of ways. For example, if old work shirts are suddenly the rage, scour the thrift stores for all you can get and have them imprinted with your youth group logo or use them as camp shirts.

Suggested classroom activities

If you wish to do a classroom activity, have small groups create and perform skits based on the subjects in the list of questions below.

Thinking through the questions

This questionnaire can stimulate discussion or lead into a Bible study on a number of topics, such as:

* Authority and our clothing (questions 3 and 4)
* What are we trying to say by the way we dress? (question 7)
* Modesty: What is it? Does it change? When have we crossed the line? (questions 13 and 14)
* Parents and clothing (questions 5-7)

My HERO

1. POLITICS Do you have a political leader you admire? If so, who is he or she?

2. SPORTS Sports have been a part of our history since our nation started. Do you have a sports hero? What is his or her name?

3. MILITARY Do you have a hero who was discovered during war? Who is he or she?

4. FILM Do you have a film star whom you especially look up to? If so, who is he or she?

5. MUSIC STAR Musicians have been adored for ages. Do you have a musical hero? If so, who is he or she?

6. ENTERTAINMENT Entertainers come in all shapes and sizes—magicians, mimes, actors, dancers, comedians. Do you have an entertainer you really look up to? If so, who is he or she?

7. FAME A famous person can come from any area. Do you have someone whose fame has captured your admiration? If so, who is he or she?

8. ACADEMIC There are many quiet intellectuals, like scientists, who inspire respect and admiration. If you have a hero from the academic community, what is his or her name?

9. WRITER/POET Writers and poets can inspire a great following. Is your hero a writer or poet? If so, who is he/she?

10. ARTIST If you look up to a great painter, sculptor, or even a cartoonist, what is his or her name?

UP CLOSE AND PERSONAL HEROES

11. In your world—home, school, church, work—is there anyone whom you really respect and who has influenced your life? If so, what is that person's name?

HOW TO USE
My Hero

Heroes play an important part in shaping kids' lives. Heroes influence your group's profile and personality—you do well to find out who those heroes are.

My Hero helps you do just that. It reveals the people your students admire and possibly follow. Secondly, it provides a natural opening for a Bible study, lesson, or series of talks on heroes. This questionnaire offers an introduction to biblical heroes, historical heroes such as Christians who impacted the world for Christ, and present-day heroes—those often-unsung men and women who quietly provide much needed influence over impressionable teenagers.

Suggested classroom activities
You can round out the questionnaire by adding one or more of these activities: Have students search magazines for photos of heroes both good and bad; have students create a list of steps young people can take that will help them develop the characteristics of a true hero; get a local hero to come and speak to your group.

Thinking through the questions
You'll notice that the questions are very straightforward; it won't take long to complete the questionnaire. Once you have the information, help your kids to identify what characteristics are shared by the people that attract your students' respect and admiration. Which of those traits do they share? Are there any they could develop? How?

My Favorite Toys

Age ___ Male ___ Female ___ Grade ___ School _____

1. Circle any of the following "toys" that you own. Underline any three that you don't have but would like to own.

Nintendo/Sega, etc.	Car	Guns
CD player	Sewing machine	Weights
Walkman	Needlepoint gear	Computer
Portable CD player	Rappelling gear	Piano
Bike	Raft	Other musical instruments
Skates	Canoe	Fishing gear
Skateboard	Kayak	Paint ball guns
Surfboard	Art supplies	Scuba gear
Bodyboard	Bowling ball	Pool table
Snow skis	Dirt bike	Foosball table
Snow board	Motorcycle	Camera
Jet ski	Golf clubs	Video camera
Water skis	Guitar	Other: _____

2. Have you ever bought something that was part of a fad?
___ Yes ___ No

3. How much do you play games?
___ Often ___ Occasionally ___ Seldom ___ Never

4. What are your three most favorite games?

1.

2.

3.

5. What is the most expensive toy you own?

Did you buy it with your own money?
___ Yes ___ No

6. Do have any toy that you are hesitant or unwilling to let others mess with?
___ Yes ___ No
If yes, which toy is it?

7. If you could only have one toy, what would it be? Why?

8. Which of your toys could be the focus of your future career?

9. What are three toys your father owns?

1.

2.

3.

10. What are three toys your mother owns?

1.

2.

3.

11. Which of your toys do you spend too much time playing with?

12. Which of the toys you listed above are you losing interest in?

13. What do you think you will do with your current favorite toy when it gets old or you lose interest in it? (circle one)
Keep it   Sell it   Give it away   Throw it away

14. Do you often buy a toy on impulse and then lose interest in it?
___ Yes ___ No

15. Which of your toys do you think takes the most skill to use?

16. Just for fun, add up the approximate prices for all of your toys and their accessories. How much does it add up to?

HOW TO USE
My Favorite Toys

What activities are your students involved in outside of the group? What material goods do they crave? Knowing the answers to these questions will help you get a feel for the levels of materialism and consumerism that exist in your students.

The information here can also give you ideas for events and outings that are likely to appeal to your group. It can help you tailor a ministry to those students with special or common interests. For example, if a number of kids indicate that they enjoy skateboarding, you can create activities just for the skaters in your group and encourage the kids to bring along friends who skate too.

Suggested classroom activities
Ask students to bring their favorites toys to the meeting; have them bring toys they used to like but now consider stupid (have a retro party); sponsor a toy drive.

Thinking through the questions
Question 1 identifies activities that have a large following among your kids. Use this information to your advantage.

Questions 4, 9, and 10 give you clues about how much and how well a kid's family may interact. For example, a family that plays games together is often more cohesive and healthier than one which does not.

Question 14 tips you off as to the impulsive nature of students.

Questions 6 and 16 give you a hint regarding the economic condition of your kids or their families.

Know It All

PLEASE PRINT!

Name _____ Age _____

Male ___ Female ___

Address _____

City _____ Zip _____

Phone _____ Date of Birth_____

1. Do you want to be taller than your father/mother?
   ___ Yes ___ No

2. What is your favorite TV program?

3. Do you have a hobby? If so, what is it?

4. What brand of deodorant do you use?

5. Do you attend a church?
   ___ Yes ___ No
   If yes, which one?

6. Do you have a pet?
   ___ Yes ___ No
   If yes, what is it?

7. Does your mom or dad go to church?
   ___ Yes ___ No ___ Sometimes

8. How many sticks of gum do you think you can chew at one time? (circle one)
   4   6   8   10   12   More than 12

9. What grade are you in?

10. Which would you rather eat? (circle one)
    Liver   Eggplant   Lima beans   Squid

11. In your opinion, what best describes the term "Christian"? (check one)
    ___ A person who goes to church
    ___ A person who believes in God
    ___ A person who lives a good life
    ___ A person who believes in the teachings of Jesus
    ___ A person who claims to be "born again"

12. What is the weirdest pizza topping you have ever eaten?

13. When is the best time to pick your nose?

14. In your opinion, is the homosexual lifestyle okay for some people?
    ___ Yes ___ No

15. What radio station do you listen to most often?

16. Do you have a favorite sport?
    ___ Yes ___ No
    If so, what is it?

17. Do you pray?
    ___Often ___Sometimes ___Seldom ___Never

18. What is your middle name?

HOW TO USE
Know It All

This questionnaire helps you get to know students who are new to you. It's light and humorous, yet provides valuable information. In addition to the basics such as mailing address and phone numbers, the answers to this questionnaire give you insight regarding interests and opinions. This knowledge will help you set the direction for your teaching.

Suggested classroom activities

Because this questionnaire is aimed primarily at new groups, a great time to use it is at a "Welcome to the Junior High Youth Group" party or similar activity. Perhaps you can make a party game out of this questionnaire. Divide the group into teams; have kids interview each other rather than filling out questionnaires themselves. The first team to finish wins. See the questions below for some silly ideas that will make this fun.

Thinking through the questions

Question 8 asks how many sticks of gum a kid can chew. Provide the gum and go for it. Question 10 mentions liver, eggplant, lima beans, and squid. Supply these (dried squid is available in ethnic sections of major food stores) and see who can eat some. Bring some pizza with strange toppings on the side (for question 12). We won't suggest a nose picking contest (see question 13).

On the serious side, questions 5 and 7 deal with an individual's church background. Will the student's parents approve of his or her involvement in your group? You also will have some insight into what to expect when you meet the parents.

Questions 2, 3, 6, 15, and 16 provide clues about where the youth's interests are. A pet, music, hobby, or sport can form a door of common interest, opening an honest opportunity to gain a meaningful relationship with this student.

By contrasting question 9 with the student's age, you can see if there is a discrepancy between the grade and the age that would be normal for that grade. This may give you a clue to both the maturity and academic level of this student.

Question 11 gives you a picture of the individual's understanding of Christianity and his or her probable relationship to Christ. Question 17 gives a hint as to how serious the individual might feel about God.

Question 14 helps you pick up some insights about the student's parents: their values and liberal or conservative leanings.

All About You!

PLEASE PRINT!

Name _____ Age _____

Male ___ Female ___

Address _____

City _____ Zip _____

Phone _____ Date of Birth_____

1. What is your grade in school? (circle one)
   6th   7th   8th   9th   10th   11th   12th

2. What school do you attend?

3. How many brothers and sisters do you have?
   ___ Brothers
   ___ Sisters

4. What is your mother's first and last name?

5. What is your father's first and last name?

6. Whom do you live with? (circle one)
   Mom   Dad   Both   Other:

7. How many years have you lived in this area?

8. Who introduced you to our church or youth program?

9. Do you have a Bible that is easy for you to read?
   ___ Yes ___ No

10. Do you drive?
    ___ Yes ___ No
    If yes, do you have a car available for your use?
    ___ Yes ___ No

11. List a few of your good friends.

12. Do you work?
    ___ Yes ___ No
    If yes, what days or evenings?

13. Do you play on any sports teams?
    ___ Yes ___ No
    If yes, what sports?

14. What hobbies or interests do you presently enjoy?

15. Are you and your folks planning to move in the near future?
    ___ Yes ___ No
    If yes, where?

HOW TO USE
All About You

This questionnaire is an information update form to use from time to time with a growing or new group. The most logical times to use this questionnaire are when new kids are added to your program or during events designed to bring new kids in.

Suggested classroom activities

This questionnaire will not take long to complete. You can use it at the beginning or end of any event or meeting. If you wish to build a meeting around it, use party games that help kids meet each other. For example, make a list of fun items that kids are supposed to learn about each other (for example, "Find someone who has never been to Disneyland"). The first person to fill out all the items, listing a different person per item, wins.

Thinking through the questions

This is a basic information questionnaire that will reveal some important facts. What school or schools are you drawing from (question 2)? Who can drive (question 10)? How can you reach parents (questions 4 and 5)? Who are the friends your students can bring into the group (question 11)?

MY YOUTH GROUP

1. I am a ___ Male ___ Female

2. What is your grade in school? (circle one)
6th   7th   8th   9th   10th   11th   12th

3. I have been in our youth group for ____ years. (circle one)
1   2   3   4   5   6

4. Most of my close friends are in our youth group.
___ Yes ___ No

5. I invite my friends to our youth programs: (check one)
___ Often ___ Sometimes ___ Rarely ___ Never

6. When it comes to youth activities, I think: (check one)
___ We have too few ___ We have enough
___ We have too many

7. I participate in our youth activities: (check one)
___ Always ___ Sometimes ___ Rarely

8. In my opinion, we need: (check one)
___ More kids in our youth group
___ To stay the same,—we are about right
___ Fewer kids—we have too many

9. In my opinion, our activities are: (check one)
___ Interesting and fun
___ Okay
___ Good enough for me
___ A little dull
___ Boring

10. I think our activities are: (check one)
___ Reasonable in price ___ Cost a lot
___ Cost too much

11. I think the singing and music in our youth group is: (check one)
___ Great ___ Okay ___ Sort of dull
___ Bad ___ We don't sing, so who cares?

12. I think that our Bible studies are: (check one)
___ Great ___ Kind of interesting ___ So-so ___ Boring

13. In my opinion we need more: (check one)
___ Teen leadership
___ Girls in leadership
___ Guys in leadership
___ Adults in leadership

14. In my opinion, we: (check one)
___ Need to be more serious about our faith
___ Need to reach out more to unbelieving kids
___ Are about the right balance of fun and serious stuff
___ Need to lighten up and have more fun

15. I keep coming to our youth group for all of the reasons I've checked below:
___ Parents
___ Fun
___ Friends
___ Activities
___ Bible studies
___ Adults I like
___ Other:

16. I would like to be in a leadership position within our youth group.
___ Yes ___ No

HOW TO USE
My Youth Group

Every leader must bite the bullet from time to time and find out how the troops feel. Do your kids like what you are doing? This questionnaire will provide the answer.

The profit from this survey will depend on three factors. First, the kids in your group will need to know that you are sincere and that you will seriously consider their opinions. Second, keep in mind that your students' opinions really do matter, even if their opinions hurt or you don't always agree with them. Kids are honest, blunt, and sometimes cruel in their appraisals. As much as it may bite, this is how the kids feel. It is important to respond in some way. Third, respond as soon as possible. If your program has serious problems, your kids will not wait long for the solutions. If some of the things kids want are impractical, explain to them the reasons why.

Suggested classroom activities

Introduce the questionnaire with a lighthearted approach by having everyone scratch each other's back. Tell your students, "We want to scratch where it itches, which means we want to know what you think of our youth program and how we can make it better and better—to scratch where you itch. That's what this questionnaire is about."

Thinking through the questions

Questions 4 and 5 reveal a kid's true attitude about your youth program: if he or she really likes it, friends will be invited. Questions 6-10 help to explain why he or she is or isn't inviting friends.

Questions 11, 12, and 13 focus on music, Bible study, and leadership. Frankly, it is better to do without music than to do it badly. And as one youth minister said, "It is a sin to bore kids with the Bible."

The answers to questions 14 and 15 will help you find the bridge to a young person's friendship. Take an interest in what they are interested in.

Question 16 will let you know if someone is leaving the group soon.

School Daze

PLEASE PRINT!

Name _____ Age _____

Male ___ Female ___

Address _____

City _____ Zip _____

Phone _____ Date of Birth_____

1. What school do you attend?

2. What time does your school start?

   What time does it end?

3. What time does your lunch start?

   What time does it end?

4. Are you involved in any extracurricular student clubs?
   ___ Yes ___ No
   If yes, which ones?

5. Does your school have any kind of Bible study or Christian group that meets on campus?
   ___ Yes ___ No
   If yes, what is it called?

   When does it meet?

   Do you attend?
   ___ Yes ___ No
   If no, would you be interested in starting one or attending?
   ___ Yes ___ No

6. Who is the principal of your school?

7. Who is your favorite teacher?

8. Who, in your opinion, is the worst teacher at your school?

9. Do you have an open campus (you can come and go when you want)?
   ___ Yes ___ No

10. What is your grade average? (circle one)
    A   B   C   D   F

11. Is your school public or private?
    ___Public ___Private

12. Are you involved in any school sports programs?
    ___ Yes ___ No
    If yes, which ones?

13. Where in school does your group hang out?

14. What is your favorite class this year?

15. What is your least favorite class this year?

16. Do you feel that you are getting a good education from your school?
    ___ Yes ___ No

17. How much time do you spend doing homework each day?

18. Do you know of any teachers who are Christians?
    ___ Yes ___ No
    If yes, please give their names.

19. Have you ever been suspended from school?
    ___ Yes ___ No

20. Do you eat in the cafeteria or buy lunch at school?
    ___ Yes ___ No

22. Do you attend school football games?
    ___ Yes ___ No ___Sometimes

23. Do you have a part-time job after school?
    ___ Yes ___ No

24. Do you have a job on the weekends?
    ___ Yes ___ No

25

HOW TO USE
School Daze

This questionnaire can be used to glean valuable information about the environment your students live in most of the day. You'll learn about the study habits and time constraints your students have. If you are thinking of working on campus, the questionnaire can give you a lead on where to go, what time things happen, and who among the staff might be a good connection.

Suggested classroom activities

Because this questionnaire focuses on school, a good time to use it is during the same week as a school rally, open house, report cards, or the like. A good discussion can be built around the contrast between typical public school values and Christian values.

Thinking through the questions

Questions 1-4 give you an outline of a student's day. If a student's schedule differs from the norm, he or she may have a special work schedule or be taking extra credit of some kind.

Questions 6, 12, 13, and 22 tell you how much this student may be involved in school life. If you have a lot of kids involved in a sports program, attendance could be affected during a particular season.

Questions 10, 14-17, and 19 give you some insight into the personal habits and attitudes of a student. You can check academic performance; you can see if the student tends to shift the blame toward the school when it is obvious (say by lack of time spent on homework) that he or she is not pulling his or her weight. You can observe the other demands that might be placed on the student such as outside work.

Questions 5 and 18 give you an idea of what is going on in the spiritual dimension on campus. It will give you the names of teachers to contact if you or your youth need a contact or sponsor on campus who is favorable toward Christianity.

SUPERSTITIONS

Check one: ___ Male ___ Female

1. I am _____ years old. (circle one)
   11 12 13 14 15 16 17 18 19 20 21+

2. Do you read horoscopes?
   ___ Daily ___ Occasionally ___ Never

3. Do you believe that horoscopes are true?
   ___ Yes ___ No ___ Not sure

4. Do you believe there is such a thing as an unlucky number?
   ___ Yes ___ No ___ Not sure

5. Would you take a seat on an airplane if it were #13?
   ___ Yes ___ No ___ Not if there was another seat

6. What do you think of hotels that skip 13 when numbering the floors—they go from 12 to 14? (check one)
   ___ They must know something I don't.
   ___ They must believe that 13 is an unlucky number.
   ___ There must be a lot of people who won't take those rooms.
   ___ The hotel management is dumb for going along with superstition.

7. Do you think Friday the 13th is an unlucky day?
   ___ Yes ___ No ___ Not sure

8. Check any of the following ideas that you think have merit.
   ___ Breaking a mirror is seven years bad luck.
   ___ Spilling salt is unlucky.
   ___ There are such things as good luck charms (rabbit foot, four-leaf clover, and so on).
   ___ Walking under a ladder is bad luck.
   ___ A black cat crossing your path is bad luck.
   ___ Knocking on wood keeps something bad from happening after you talk about it.

9. Do you believe that people can tell your future with tea leaves, palm reading, tarot cards, and so forth?
   ___ Yes ___ No ___ Not sure

10. Do you ever play with an Ouija board?
    ___ Yes ___ No ___ Not sure

11. Do you think Ouija boards really work?
    ___ Yes ___ No ___ Not sure

12. Do you believe in ghosts?
    ___ Yes ___ No ___ Not sure

13. Do you believe that some homes are haunted?
    ___ Yes ___ No ___ Not sure

14. Do you carry a rabbit's foot or any other kind of good-luck charm?
    ___ Yes ___ No

15. Do you believe that some people can cast spells on other people?
    ___ Yes ___ No

HOW TO USE
Superstitions

Many kids, even longtime churchgoers, can be superstitious. The purpose of this questionnaire is to help you discover the degree of superstition in your group's attenders, the areas where superstition is most prevalent, and at which age level and in which gender the subject is given high attention.

A perfect time to use this questionnaire is on Friday the thirteenth (or the thirteenth of any month).

Suggested classroom activities

Use this questionnaire as an opener to a study of Saul and the medium of Endor (1 Samuel 28:7-25), Simon the magician (Acts 8:9-25), or a Christmas Bible study about the wise men (who were really astrologers).

Do a Bible study about luck and the sovereignty of God. Deal with the subject of the occult, particularly if kids respond strongly to the questions about fortune telling and Ouija boards. If the kids believe in ghosts, teach about what happens to a person after death.

Bring in horoscopes and other items mentioned by the questionnaire to use as visual aids.

Thinking through the questions

The questions cover several main areas of superstition. The ability to predict the future or answer questions is covered by questions 2 and 3 (horoscopes) and 9-11 (Ouija boards, tea leaves, and so on). Unlucky omens (the number 13, broken mirrors, black cats, and the like) are touched on in questions 4-8 and 14. Ghosts get the treatment in questions 12 and 13. Question 15 talks of casting spells (witchcraft and the satanic).

The answers to these questions will tell you which areas need to be addressed in your teaching.

WHO IS A MISSIONARY?

1. Missionaries are Christians who work in the jungle with primitive people.
___ Yes ___ No ___Sometimes

2. Missionaries are specialists in the Christian church.
___ Yes ___ No ___Sometimes

3. A real missionary is someone who plants churches, teaches, or preaches to natives in another country.
___ Yes ___ No ___Sometimes

4. Missionaries can work here in our country and still be called missionaries.
___ Yes ___ No

5. Missionaries always have to know another language.
___ Yes ___ No

6. Missionaries are specially educated, trained, and equipped people.
___ Yes ___ No ___Sometimes

7. Missionaries are called by God because they are super-spiritual people.
___ Yes ___ No ___ Not sure

8. To become a missionary, a person must be led by God in some unusual way, like a dream or a vision.
___ Yes ___ No

9. Missionaries are average Christians who love God and want to take his message to other people who haven't heard.
___ Yes ___ No ___Sometimes

10. How do missionaries get their money? (check all that apply)
___ They ask for it.
___ They trust God for it.
___ They are paid by their church.
___ They are paid by their denomination or mission agency.
___ They receive gifts in the mail.
___ They receive gifts from those they work with.
___ They win the lottery.

11. Missionaries have high-risk jobs.
___ Always ___ Sometimes ___ Never

12. Most foreign missionaries come home for a year after:
___ Two years
___ Three years
___ Four years
___ Eight years
___ Never

13. Missionaries are often asked to tell about their work in church meetings. Rate the missionaries you have heard:
___ Generally good speakers
___ Average speakers
___ Boring
___ I've never heard one

14. I know the names of one or more missionaries sent or supported by my church.
___ Yes ___ No

15. Missionaries can have jobs like carpenters, school teachers, pilots, secretaries, graphic artists, accountants, etc.
___ Yes ___ No

16. I have met a missionary and talked with him or her.
___ Yes ___ No

17. My family helps to support a missionary.
___ Yes ___ No

18. I would like to become a missionary.
___ Yes ___ No

Who Is a Missionary?

This questionnaire forms a natural basis to begin a lesson or series of lessons on missionaries and their work.

When most kids think of the term missionary, they form an image of some poor soul out in the jungles, swatting bugs and translating the Bible. You have the opportunity to expand your students' concepts. Mission fields and mission works come in all shapes and sizes. Furthermore, you can make your kids aware that all Christians are called to do the work of a missionary, pointing others to the Lord.

Is a potential missionary lurking in your youth group? The answer is yes.

Suggested classroom activities

If your students do not have a good grasp on what missionaries are like or what they do, it's time to introduce them to mission work through a missionary on furlough or by taking them to a work in progress at home or in the foreign field. Your denomination can supply relevant information.

Build a Bible study on the Great Commission (Matthew 28:18-20) or on Jesus' call in Acts 1:8.

Thinking through the questions

The correct answers (to the questions that have them) are listed below. The comments that follow offer deeper explanations.

Question 1: Sometimes	Question 8: No
Question 2: Sometimes	Question 9: Yes
Question 3: Sometimes	Question 10: All answers okay
Question 4: Yes	Question 11: Sometimes
Question 5: No	Question 12: Three years
Question 6: Sometimes	Question 15: Yes
Question 7: No	

One important truth about mission work that your students should gain as you discuss the subject is: Any person with a usable skill can become a full-time missionary. In fact, mission fields are calling for typists, mechanics, medical specialists, builders, dorm parents, teachers, and much more. Questions 1-6 and 15 help to point out that missionaries can work in any part of the world, including right here at home, and that mission work comes in many forms. Questions 7 and 8 allow you to discuss the fact that all Christians are called to do missionary work daily (see Matthew 28:18-20). Question 11 opens a great opportunity to tell some of the exciting stories of the adventures some missionaries experience in their fields.

MY GREATEST FEARS

For each question below, check the one answer that most nearly describes your reaction.

1. Suppose you were embarrassed in front of your whole school student body. How would you feel?
___ Devastated   ___ Humiliated
___ I would wish I were dead   ___ Angry
___ Bitter   ___ I can take it

2. When you are asked to speak publicly, what is your reaction?
___ No way
___ Scared
___ Nervous
___ Uncomfortable
___ Pretty cool
___ In control

3. How do you look at the idea of marriage?
___ Panic
___ Major fear
___ Overwhelming
___ I can cut it
___ Great

4. How would feel if you were raped, sexually assaulted, or sexually molested?
___ I can't even think about it!
___ I'd want to die
___ Devastated
___ I would do the best I could to cope
___ I could get over it eventually
___ I could forgive

5. How would you react if you were arrested and jailed?
___ Devastated
___ Bitter
___ I could live with it
___ Make the best of it

6. How would you react if your family lost everything and had to live on the street?
___ I would want to die
___ Devastated
___ Bitter
___ Make the best of it

7. How would you feel if you were kidnaped?
___ Fearful
___ Panicky
___ Angry
___ I would stay in control
___ I would make the best of it

8. How would you react if your parents were killed in an accident?
___ I would want to die too
___ Devastated
___ Bitter at God
___ Empty and lost
___ I would work through it
___ I would make the best of it

9. How would you feel if you were paralyzed in a major accident?
___ I won't think about it!
___ I would want to die
___ Devastated
___ Bitter at God
___ I would make the best of it

10. How would you feel if you knew you had only months to live?
___ Devastated
___ Majorly depressed
___ Bitter at God
___ I would know it was my time to go

11. How do you feel about your own death?
___ Terrified
___ Worst possible thing
___ Scared
___ All have to go some day
___ Some apprehension
___ I'm not afraid of death
___ I'm excited about heaven

12. How do you think you would handle terrible physical or emotional pain?
___ No way!
___ I would rather die
___ Pain scares me
___ I can handle it to a point
___ I could tough it out

13. List your four greatest fears.

     1.

     2.

     3.

     4.

HOW TO USE
My Greatest Fears

A questionnaire like this can reveal a lot about what is inside individuals and inside your group. The answers will reveal the greatest perceived fears of the group. You'll find several areas of fear that need to be dealt with in your group. Questions like these will prompt other good, honest questions. Also, this questionnaire can be a great basis for a Bible study or lesson on dealing with fear.

WARNING: Handle this topic with extreme sensitivity. It is not at all unusual to discover that someone in the group has been raped, been in an accident, suffered the death of a parent, or faced other significant pain.

Suggested classroom activities
A good time for a look at fear is during Halloween week or after a tragedy strikes in your youth group.

Distribute newspapers and have small groups cut out scary headlines to discuss. Talk about recent scary movies as a lead-in to the subject. Conduct a Bible study on the power of God to overcome fear.

Thinking through the questions
The subjects covered by the questions, in order, are embarrassment, public speaking, marriage, rape, jail, poverty, being kidnaped, being orphaned, major accidents, fatal disease, death, and pain. One of the responses a student can circle in several of the questions is "bitter at God." Talk about your students' views of God. Is he a merciless judge? Does he care when his children suffer? Is he to be feared? Is he angry at us?

What's Really Important?

Read this questionnaire through once without answering. Then circle a response to each situation that indicates how important you think it is.

1. **Helping street people in our community**
   Urgent need   Great need   Somewhat of a need
   Little need   No need

2. **Helping street people in big cities**
   Urgent need   Great need   Somewhat of a need
   Little need   No need

3. **Helping people with AIDS**
   Urgent need   Great need   Somewhat of a need
   Little need   No need

4. **Helping starving children and adults in Africa**
   Urgent need   Great need   Somewhat of a need
   Little need   No need

5. **Helping people endangered in warring countries**
   Urgent need   Great need   Somewhat of a need
   Little need   No need

6. **Saving endangered species like whales and elephants**
   Urgent need   Great need   Somewhat of a need
   Little need   No need

7. **Ministering to people who are locked up in prisons and penitentiaries**
   Urgent need   Great need   Somewhat of a need
   Little need   No need

8. **Rescuing foreign missionaries held hostage by guerrillas**
   Urgent need   Great need   Somewhat of a need
   Little need   No need

9. **Helping orphans in orphanages around the world**
   Urgent need   Great need   Somewhat of a need
   Little need   No need

10. **Teaching those who cannot read and write**
    Urgent need   Great need   Somewhat of a need
    Little need   No need

11. **Sharing Jesus with those who have never heard the gospel**
    Urgent need   Great need   Somewhat of a need
    Little need   No need

Go back and put a star by those whom you would help with your time and resources.

HOW TO USE
What's Really Important?

This questionnaire has two primary uses. First, the answers given by your students will reveal to some extent the degree and direction of your group's compassion. Second, the answers will form a good basis for a discussion on worldwide needs and where you as a group can get involved.

Suggested classroom activities

A prayer meeting based on the areas of need your students will consider is a great activity. Decide who will pray for which subject and what specifically should be prayed.

Your class can discuss tangible things they might do to help the needy. For example, they might plan a hospital visitation day or raise money to sponsor an orphan.

Thinking through the questions

The topics covered by the questions are, in order, street people, AIDS patients, the starving, war victims, endangered species, prisoners, missionary hostages, orphans, the illiterate, and the unsaved.

Your students will likely be most concerned about whatever the newspapers and TV are currently emphasizing (which won't be missionary hostages or the unsaved). The answers will help you see what the kids are really interested in. Emphasize the areas your students are least interested in; those are the areas of which they are most ignorant and need some education.

TALK WALKERS

Please fill out the questions below with the names of kids in our youth group. Do not use your own name nor that of anyone who is not a regular attender of our group. You can use a name more than once.

1. Write the names of one guy and one girl you would go to if you wanted someone to pray for you.

2. Write the names of one guy and one girl you would go to if you had a question about the Bible or spiritual things.

3. Write the names of one guy and one girl whose lives are examples of Christian love.

4. Write the names of one guy and one girl who are unafraid to declare their faith.

5. Write the names of one guy and one girl who are good examples of how a Christian should live in the real world.

6. Write the names of one guy and one girl who are friendly and warm towards new kids.

7. Write the names of one guy and one girl you feel would give you wise, godly advice about things going on in your life.

8. Write the names of one guy and one girl who each have a family life that you admire.

9. Write the names of one guy and one girl you think are spiritual leaders in our group.

10. Write the names of one guy and one girl who have good self-discipline.

11. Write the names of one guy and one girl whom you could go to if you were in trouble.

HOW TO USE
Talk Walkers

This simple questionnaire can be used to tell you whom the kids see as the vibrant spiritual leaders of the youth group. Pay attention; what they say is bound to be pretty accurate.

Jot down the names of kids listed, and note who are mentioned the most. If someone shines in a particular area, note that as well. This knowledge will help you select leaders for your youth group or ministry team. You'll discover which students to put special effort and work into and whom to encourage with personal letters that describe the way their peers rated them in spiritual leadership. You will know which kids to use for specialty programs such as missions, discipleship, or evangelism. Finally, you will be able to place kids in positions for which they have interest, ability, and aptitude.

Suggested classroom activities

You may wish to provide a list or have students compose a list of names of the regular members of your group. This way, all of the students working on the questionnaire are focused on the same people.

Work with your students to define leadership. Some of the key characteristics to consider are authority, dependability, wisdom, integrity, and spirituality.

Thinking through the questions

Though the questions are straightforward, allow plenty of time for students to mull over their answers. Be prepared to define or give examples of the key concepts in each question. Question 3, for instance, may cause students to wonder what examples of Christian love are.

The subjects covered are, in order: prayer, the Bible, Christian love, witnessing, Christian living, friendliness, godly advice, family life, spiritual leadership, self-discipline, and help in times of trouble.

Give It Up

1. About how much money do you earn or receive each week? (circle one)

   None $5 $10 $20 $30 $50 $100 or more

2. How do you get your money? (circle all that apply)

   Allowance   Job   Baby-sitting   Other:

3. Do you have to do chores to earn your allowance?
   ___ Yes ___ No

4. How would you describe your family's financial condition? (circle one)

   Rather poor   Fairly average   Well-off   Wealthy

5. Do you think you should have more allowance or a salary increase?
   ___ Yes ___ No

6. Are you buying anything on time payments (credit)?
   ___ Yes ___ No

7. Do you have your own checking account?
   ___ Yes ___ No

8. Do you have your own savings account?
   ___ Yes ___ No

9. Are you saving money on a regular basis?
   ___ Yes ___ No

10. Do your parents require you to help pay room and board at your home?
    ___ Yes ___ No

11. Do you have your own credit card?
    ___ Yes ___ No

12. Do you use your parents' credit card?
    ___ Yes ___ No

13. Do you regularly give money to your church, a charity, or a missionary?
    ___ Yes ___ No

14. What's the next item you plan to purchase?

15. As you think of the future, is money very important to you?
    ___ Yes ___ So-so ___ No

16. Are you ever tempted to steal?
    ___ Yes ___ No

17. About how much money do you usually carry with you?

18. Do you often buy things impulsively?
    ___ Yes ___ No

19. Do you often borrow money from friends?
    ___ Yes ___ No
    If yes, do you pay them back promptly?
    ___ Yes ___ Usually ___ No

20. Do you often regret that you have bought an item shortly after you purchased it?
    ___ Yes ___ No

21. Do you ever find yourself holding back money from the church or youth group offering because you want to use it to purchase some other item?
    ___ Yes ___ No

HOW TO USE
Give It Up

What do your students know about money? Where do they get their money and what do they buy? Do they handle their finances in a wise and godly manner? It pays to know the answers because money is a chief priority to each of your students. It can be a blessing or a snare.

This questionnaire has three purposes: first, to let you know how your students think about and use money; second, to form a springboard for a Bible study or lesson on how to handle money; third, to encourage your kids to use their money wisely.

Suggested classroom activities

As mentioned above, you can do a lesson on stewardship. The parable of the talents is a natural.

Tithing is a good subject; perhaps your class would be willing to collect money over a period of time for a worthy cause.

There's the good ol' "burn the five dollar bill" object lesson (burn it a little each time until it no longer has value—a lesson on wasting one's life).

Thinking through the questions

How important is the value of a dollar? Many of the questions—especially those that ask how students earn money, how well-off they are, whether they borrow, buy on credit, or shop impulsively—will let you know what your students think. You can get an idea of how much (or how little) a student's Christian beliefs impact his or her spending habits with questions 13 and 21. Work ethic is covered in questions 3, 10, 12, 16, and 19. The kid who is willing to work hard for a reward is likely to be an asset to your ministry.

Am I a Leader?

Name _____ Date _____

I. I want to be a leader because—(check as many as strongly apply)

___ I like to be someone that others respect and look up to
___ I want to learn to be a leader
___ I like to be in control
___ I want to be part of the leadership group
___ I can make a contribution to the program
___ I don't want to be a leader
___ Other:

II. Rate yourself in each of the following areas by circling the appropriate number.

1. My energy level (10 = I am very energetic all the time)
   1   2   3   4   5   6   7   8   9   10

2. My commitment level (10 = I always finish what I start)
   1   2   3   4   5   6   7   8   9   10

3. My example (10 = I am a consistent model, one who sets the pace)
   1   2   3   4   5   6   7   8   9   10

4. I can accept authority over me (10 = No problem)
   1   2   3   4   5   6   7   8   9   10

5. My common sense (10 = I am able to see and accomplish simple solutions to common problems)
   1   2   3   4   5   6   7   8   9   10

6. My self-discipline (10 = I am self-disciplined)
   1   2   3   4   5   6   7   8   9   10

7. My cool-headedness (10 = I have the ability to stay calm under pressure)
   1   2   3   4   5   6   7   8   9   10

8. My loyalty (10 = I am loyal)
   1   2   3   4   5   6   7   8   9   10

9. My team player factor (10 = I am a strong team player)
   1   2   3   4   5   6   7   8   9   10

10. My ability to communicate (10 = I am able to speak clearly and convincingly)
    1   2   3   4   5   6   7   8   9   10

11. My creativity (10 = I am creative)
    1   2   3   4   5   6   7   8   9   10

12. My teachability (10 = I am teachable and able to learn new things)
    1   2   3   4   5   6   7   8   9   10

HOW TO USE
Am I a Leader?

Use this questionnaire with your youth staff or with those who desire to work with youth.

The primary benefit of this evaluation is to help your volunteers uncover areas in which they need improvement, encouragement, and training. This will aid you, the leader, in gaining a better understanding of the strong and weak points of your team.

You will need to describe the meaning of each question in detail while your people are working as described in *Thinking through the questions* below.

Suggested classroom activities

This questionnaire should be utilized at a leadership planning meeting. Be sure to communicate what your program is all about and what you need in the way of staff. As your volunteers work on the questions, warn them not to become discouraged as they uncover weak areas. Knowing where we are more likely to fail is the first step in strengthening our defenses to prevent failure.

Thinking through the questions

Section I focuses on the motives of leadership. Point out to your people that leadership involves servanthood; it is not always a glamorous thing.

Section II deals with the energy level required to be a leader in youth work. A person with little energy or stamina will have trouble in a high-energy program.

Question 2 hinges on the essential qualities of commitment and dedication. Be sure to outline the commitment you're asking your staff to make. Have an end point to any job; you can always pick up the person's "option."

Question 3 focuses on a worker's personal example or testimony. God wants servants who model the truth.

Question 4 speaks of the flip side of leadership; the ability to take orders and to submit to others.

Question 5 takes a look at a person's ability to use the ol' noggin. This is the ability to discern a simple solution and do it.

Question 6 looks at self-discipline: the ability to make yourself do what must be done or should be done, even though you don't want to do it.

Question 7 deals with the ability to remain calm under pressure. All leaders need to be "cool" people—able to curb impulsive or overly emotional behavior.

Question 8 considers loyalty to the organization, group, and program. A leader loses respect and usefulness when he or she fights against the program or the leadership.

Question 9 looks at the problem raised by leaders who desire to be independent.

Question 10 deals with the ability to clearly get a message across to others. The better the leader communicates, the better his or her leadership. Much of the ability to communicate is learned through experience.

Question 11 focuses on creativity. If we can't do it one way, we must do it another way. Finding another way is creativity.

Question 12 speaks of teachability: the desire and ability to stretch and flex. Teaching comes in a variety of shapes and sizes—criticism others give us, mistakes we make, class sessions we sit in. All are opportunities to learn and grow.

How Much Do You Know About Your Faith?

1. You must be baptized in order to be a Christian.
___ Yes ___ No

2. The best definition of grace is: (check one)
___ A prayer said at mealtime
___ Something kind, gentle, and sweet
___ Getting something you don't deserve
___ God's sympathy or compassion

3. You cannot be sure that you are really saved until Judgment Day.
___ Can ___ Can't

4. The word "trinity" is found in the Bible.
___ Yes ___ No

5. Jesus was in existence before he was born in Bethlehem.
___ Yes ___ No

6. The best definition of repentance is: (check one)
___ Being sorry for what you did wrong
___ Turning and going the other way
___ Making up for all the wrong you have done
___ Telling God you are sorry in an overt, emotional way

7. Blasphemy of the Holy Spirit is the only sin that cannot be forgiven.
___ Yes ___ No

8. The Bible forbids Christians to drink alcoholic beverages.
___ Yes ___ No

9. A person can be a follower of both Christ and Buddha.
___ Yes ___ No

10. A minister or missionary is closer to God than "ordinary" Christians.
___ Yes ___ No

11. If a person was as bad as Hitler, but eventually sincerely asked Christ to be his or her Lord, that person would go to heaven.
___ Yes ___ No

12. No one has ever seen God the Father.
___ Some have ___ No one has

13. Jesus was 100 percent man and 100 percent God.
___ Yes ___ No

14. All people are born with the stain of sin upon them.
___ Yes ___ No

15. People become angels when they die.
___ Yes ___ No

16. Jesus was taken to Egypt as a small child.
___ Yes ___ No

17. Three wise men visited Christ shortly after his birth.
___ Yes ___ No

18. Jesus was known to get angry.
___ Yes ___ No

19. After his death and resurrection, how long did Jesus appear to people before he ascended to heaven? (circle one)
3 days   20 days   40 days   50 days

How Much Do You Know About Your Faith?

Do your students have a good basic knowledge of biblical truth? If they don't, they will have a hard time doing well on this questionnaire! And if they don't, that will be your signal to implement a discipleship program or Bible study series to address the need.

Suggested classroom activities

After your group has finished the questionnaire, go over the correct answers one by one. It's a good idea to ask students to give examples to support their answers. For example, if someone says that Jesus did get angry (question 18), ask for an instance (like John 2). This will help to weed out the kids who are only guessing. Some questions may trigger discussion or allow you to explain or expand with additional information.

Here's another way to go over the answers: Play a game of Sword Drill featuring the Scriptures listed in the section below. To play Sword Drill, assemble two teams and seat them one on each side of the room. Call out a Scripture reference. The first person to find it in the Bible stands up and reads the passage. He or she gets to choose someone on the other team to go out of the game. The first team to chase out all the other team's players wins the game.

Thinking through the questions

Question 1: No. The thief on the cross was not baptized (see Luke 23:39-43).
Question 2: Getting something you don't deserve. See Ephesians 1:7-8.
Question 3: Can. See 1 John 5:11-12.
Question 4: No.
Question 5: Yes. See John 8:56-58.
Question 6: Turning and going the other way.
Question 7: Yes. See Matthew 12:31.
Question 8: No. See 1 Timothy 5:23.
Question 9: No. See John 14:6; Acts 4:12.
Question 10: No, not necessarily.
Question 11: Yes. For example, the thief on the cross (see Luke 23:39-43) and the apostle Paul (see Acts 9:1-2).
Question 12: No one has. See 1 Timothy 6:15-16.
Question 13: Yes. See John 1:1,14; Philippians 2:5-7; Hebrews 2:14.
Question 14: Yes. See Romans 5:12,19.
Question 15: No. Scripture never indicates this.
Question 16: Yes. See Matthew 2:13-15.
Question 17: No. The number is never given.
Question 18: Yes. See John 2:14-16.
Question 19: Forty days. See Acts 1:3.

Happy Camper

Age ____ Male ____ Female ____

1. Have you been to camp with us before?
   ___ Yes ___ No

2. Would you like to stay at this camp a little longer?
   ___ Yes ___ No

3. How was the food?
   ___ Great ___ Good ___ Average ___ Poor

4. How did you like the fun stuff (sports, games, and the like)?
   ___ Great ___ Good ___ Average ___ Poor

5. Did you participate in most of the fun activities?
   ___ Yes ___ No

6. How did you like this camp facility?
   ___ Great ___ Good ___ Average ___ Poor

7. How did you like your cabin or living facilities?
   ___ Great ___ Good ___ Average ___ Poor

8. How did you like your counselor?
   ___ Great ___ Good ___ Average ___ Poor

9. Did you learn much from your cabin devotions?
   ___ Yes ___ No

10. How would you rate the main speaker?
    ___ Great ___ Good ___ Average ___ Poor

11. How would you rate the seminars you attended?
    ___ Great ___ Good ___ Average ___ Poor

12. What did you think about the rules?
    ___ Too many ___ Not enough ___ Just right

13. What was the activity you liked best?

14. What was the activity you liked least?

15. What was the meeting you liked best?

16. What was the meeting you liked least?

17. Did you ask any friends to come to camp this year?
    ___ Yes ___ No

18. Do you think there was too much leisure time?
    ___ Yes ___ No

19. Did you get bored?
    ___ Yes ___ No

20. Do you think there was too much going on?
    ___ Yes ___ No

21. Would you have liked more free time?
    ___ Yes ___ No

22. How would you rate the music?
    ___ Great ___ Good ___ Average ___ Poor

23. What, if anything, would you add or subtract from the music?

24. Did your friends like camp this year?
    ___ Yes ___ No

25. Did your counselor seem to like camp?
    ___ Yes ___ No

26. Do you plan on coming again next year?
    ___ Yes ___ No
    Why or why not?

27. Did you make a spiritual decision at camp this year?
    ___ Yes ___ No
    If so, please describe your decision.

HOW TO USE
Happy Camper

What makes a successful camping experience? It ranges from small things like good food to big things like spiritual growth. Use this questionnaire to evaluate the success of your latest youth camp. Who attended camp? How many made commitments to Christ? How was the main speaker received? How did your counselors do? What can improve your next camp? These and other questions will steer you toward greater and greater success.

Use this questionnaire immediately following the conclusion of camp.

Suggested classroom activities

Show your camp video or pass around photos you took at camp; have the campers make photo posters with silly labels to hang in the youth room; have students write to pen pals they met at camp.

Ask a few campers who were particularly touched by God to tell about their experiences.

Thinking through the questions

Camp was probably a success if your campers want to stay longer (question 2) and hope to return (question 26).

Questions 3-7 deal with the campers' responses to the food, facilities, and fun. Note: The best way to check if the campers enjoyed the food at camp is to check the trash cans after meals to see how much and what kind of food was thrown away.

Questions 8-11 will tell you if your staff was successful in relating to your campers. If campers have a negative attitude toward counselors (question 8), see if the counselors also had negative attitudes (question 25).

Activities and music are handled in questions 13-16 and 18-23.

Question 27 is the critical one. Did your campers draw closer to God because of camp? As you likely know, the mountain-top experiences of camp can quickly wear off in the harsh reality of life's normal routine. Focus your attention on those kids who made commitments; some of those decisions will last a lifetime.

Happy Counselor

Name _____ Date _____

1. Was our camp a good one for you?
___ Yes ___ No

2. Was it a good one for your campers?
___ Yes ___ No

3. How would you rate your cabin of kids? (circle one)
Great   Good   Overactive   Lazy   Rebels   Uncontrollable

4. How many kids did you have in your cabin?

5. How many, if any, made a commitment of some sort to Christ?

6. Did you give the names of those who made decisions to your youth minister?
___ Yes ___ No

7. How would you rate the activities and fun part of this camp? (circle one)
Great   Good   Average   Poor

8. How well did the staff handle discipline and control? (circle one)
Great   Good   Average   Poor

9. How would you rate the speaker? (circle one)
Great   Good   Average   Poor

10. How well did the main speaker relate to your campers? (circle one)
Great   Good   Average   Poor

11. Was the speaker a good communicator?
___ Yes ___ No
___ Yes, but not for the age level of the campers

12. How relevant do you think the speaker was to your kids' world? (circle one)
Very   Somewhat   Not at all

13. Were the seminars/workshops relevant?
___ Yes ___ No

14. In your opinion, how was the pace of the camp? (circle one)
Too fast   Just right   Too slow   Boring

15. Were the rules and regulations clearly stated and fair?
___ Yes ___ No

16. Were the rules and regulations too tight and hard to enforce?
___ Yes ___ No

17. Were the rules and regulations too loose and liberal?
___ Yes ___ No

18. Would you be interested in returning to this camp as a counselor next year?
___ Yes ___ No
Why or why not?

19. What would make this a better camp next year?

HOW TO USE
Happy Counselor

Camp counselors are the soldiers—the ones who build personal friendships with the kids. Their opinions of your camp can tell you a lot about how well things went and how to improve your camps in the future.

Suggested classroom activities

When your counselors are gathered together, have each share his or her experiences at camp, both good and bad. Be sure to get details on kids who made decisions and those who expressed needs you should address.

Thinking through the questions

Question 1, which deals with the counselors' personal attitudes toward camp, is a good one to open up discussion. Ask everyone to explain in detail why they did or did not enjoy various aspects of the camp. Keep notes to help you make adjustments for your next camp.

Question 3 is another good discussion question. Ask your counselors what could be done to motivate lazy kids or control overactive ones.

GIVER OR TAKER?

1. Do you contribute your time or energy to any ministry of the church?
   ___ Yes ___ No ___ Sometimes

2. Do you try to meet new kids and make them feel welcome and part of the group?
   ___ Yes ___ No ___ Sometimes

3. Do you look for opportunities to share the message of Christ with non-Christian kids?
   ___ Yes ___ No ___ Sometimes

4. Do you have anyone that you are trying to disciple and help grow as a Christian?
   ___ Yes ___ No
   If yes, who?

5. Do you help clean up on church work days, help in the child care program, or help in any other area where assistance is needed?
   ___ Yes ___ No ___ Sometimes

6. Do you give money to help the work of Christ through the church?
   ___ Yes ___ No ___ Sometimes

7. Do you give money to any ministries that help the poor?
   ___ Yes ___ No ___ Sometimes

8. Do you use any of your skills or talents to further the message of Christ?
   ___ Yes ___ No ___ I would like to but I don't know how

9. Do you read the Bible on your own?
   ___ Yes ___ No ___ Sometimes

10. Do you contribute ideas and innovations to the work of the church?
    ___ Yes ___ No ___ Sometimes

11. Do you wait to be told what needs to be done or do you take the initiative?
    ___ Wait ___ Take the initiative

12. Do you make gathering together with believers a priority—or do other things such as work, friends, school, sports, and play sometimes get in the way?
    ___ Top priority ___ Not top

13. Do you express gratitude and appreciation to those who do things for you?
    ___ Yes ___ No ___ Sometimes

14. Do you pray for the leadership of the church and those who work with kids in your age group?
    ___ Yes ___ No ___ Sometimes

15. After filling out this form would you say you are more of a "giver" or a "taker" in the body of Christ?
    ___ Giver ___ Taker ___ Not sure

Now go back and circle the areas you would like to work on changing.

HOW TO USE
Giver or Taker?

This questionnaire is designed to help your students evaluate how much of a contribution they are making to the life of the church. It will spur them on to deeper commitment and action. Use it with believers.

Suggested classroom activities

This questionnaire can be part of a lesson on servanthood, selflessness, or faith and works. Use it as an introduction to an opportunity to serve or to become part of a giving ministry. Use it to make them aware of the opportunities of service that your church has available. Sign up interested kids.

Thinking through the questions

Are any of your students working in evangelism and discipleship? Those topics are covered in questions 2, 3, 4, and 8.

Questions 1, 5, and 11 deal with general service in the church.

Questions 6 and 7 ask about the giving of money to support various ministries.

Bible study, fellowship, and prayer are covered in questions 9, 12, and 14.

Questions 10 and 13 reveal a student's attitude: Supportive or critical, appreciative or not.

At the end of the questionnaire, students are instructed to go back and circle any areas they would like to work on changing. This will give them a moment to think about how they can more deeply commit themselves to the work of Christ.

CHURCH CONNECTION

1. I attend our church service: (circle one)
   Often   Sometimes   Seldom   Never

2. My father attends our church service: (circle one)
   Often   Sometimes   Seldom   Never

3. My mother attends our church service: (circle one)
   Often   Sometimes   Seldom   Never

4. My father or mother has responsibility and/or a leadership position at the church.
   ___ Yes ___ No

5. I have to sit with my parents in church.
   ___ Yes ___ No

6. I have to attend our church service—I don't particularly want to.
   ___ Yes ___ No

7. I take communion in our church.
   ___ Yes ___ No

8. I attend another church's service: (circle one)
   Often   Sometimes   Seldom   Never

9. In my Christian life, the church service is: (circle one)
   Very important   A little important   Not important

10. The music in our church service is: (circle one)
    Great   Upbeat   Okay   For old folks   Dull and boring

11. The messages given in our church service are: (circle one)
    Great   Pretty good   Okay
    Over my head   Dull and boring

12. I'd say that our church service is: (circle one)
    Wild and exciting   Unpredictable   Informal
    Just right for me   Traditional   Formal
    Long and boring

13. Our church sanctuary or meeting room is: (circle one)
    New and modern   Beautiful   Clean
    Nice   Inviting   Warm   Functional
    Impersonal   Old   Unkempt

14. The adults in our church seem: (circle one)
    Friendly   Wise   Old   Distant

15. The adults in our church put a high priority on the youth who attend.
    ___ Yes ___ No

16. Young people or young adults get a chance to participate in the church service.
    ___ Often ___ Occasionally ___ Never

17. If I were to invite one of my friends to our church service, he/she would enjoy it.
    ___ Yes ___ No ___ On certain occasions

18. I would come to church more often if:

HOW TO USE
Church Connection

On occasion we are asked, "Why don't the kids attend the church service?" We need the right answers. This survey will give you an honest perspective on what your kids like or don't like about your church service.

When the questionnaires are complete, try to spot any trends or patterns and take action. If the church leadership wants kids to support the worship service, it may mean making changes needed to interest kids.

A survey like this should be taken on a regular basis.

Suggested classroom activities

When ready to begin, introduce the topic by saying something like, "This survey will tell us what you think of our church service. Can we make our church services more attractive to teens? Your answers will help us learn how."

A lesson on the church would be in order, using the results of the questionnaire as the basis of your study. Consult your church leaders to learn the history behind the traditions your worship service incorporates. Have your minister come and talk about your church's vision and the youth's place within that vision.

Thinking through the questions

Questions 1-9 let you know if a particular respondent is strongly or weakly involved in the life of your church. Give more weight to those who are strongly involved.

Music, preaching, the service's atmosphere, and the nature of the meeting room are covered in Questions 10-13. These are fundamentally important to the overall impression a service makes. There are two things that can be done to improve any weak spots: You can influence those who can make changes in the service (by showing them a stack of these questionnaires) and you can help your youth more clearly understand why things are as they are.

Questions 14-17 deal with the relationships between the adults and the youth in your church. Be a cheerleader for your youth! Encourage your leadership to make the youth an important part of your church's vision.

Take particular note of question 18. What would make your church service more attractive to your teens?

My **Strong** & Weak Spots

Name (optional) _____

<table>
<tr><td>

MY POSSIBLE STRENGTHS

1. I have a good personality.
___ Yes ___ No ___ So-so

2. I like people.
___ Yes ___ No ___ So-so

3. I like to work; I like to get things done.
___ Yes ___ No ___ So-so

4. I feel I'm a leader; I like to lead; people follow me.
___ Yes ___ No ___ So-so

5. When I start something, I usually finish it.
___ Yes ___ No ___ So-so

6. I can sing or play a musical instrument pretty well.
___ Yes ___ No ___ So-so

7. I'm a thinker; I have a good mind; I think things through.
___ Yes ___ No ___ So-so

8. I like art; I like to draw or paint.
___ Yes ___ No ___ So-so

9. I'm athletic; I really like sports and outdoor activities.
___ Yes ___ No ___ So-so

10. I like acting, comedy, drama, etc.
___ Yes ___ No ___ So-so

11. I like to work with my hands; I like to build stuff.
___ Yes ___ No ___ So-so

</td><td>

MY POSSIBLE WEAKNESSES

1. I have a temper with a short fuse.
___ Yes ___ No ___ So-so

2. I sometimes brag and stretch the truth in my favor.
___ Yes ___ No ___ So-so

3. I get jealous easily.
___ Yes ___ No ___ So-so

4. I have a tendency to be deceptive with unpleasant truths.
___ Yes ___ No ___ So-so

5. I hold grudges.
___ Yes ___ No ___ So-so

6. I often see the negative side.
___ Yes ___ No ___ So-so

7. I'm lazy; I just like to sit around and watch.
___ Yes ___ No ___ So-so

8. I tend to cut down or be critical of people.
___ Yes ___ No ___ So-so

9. I have a hard time keeping my word.
___ Yes ___ No ___ So-so

10. I procrastinate; I'm always putting things off.
___ Yes ___ No ___ So-so

</td></tr>
</table>

HOW TO USE
My Strong & Weak Spots

Knowing the strengths and weaknesses of your kids can be a great benefit. Placing people in positions that let them use their strengths and gifts means the jobs get done faster and better. Putting workers to work, artists to create art, and leaders in leadership makes sense. But how do we know who really likes to work, make posters, or lead? That's where this questionnaire can help!

Suggested classroom activities

Introduce the topic of strengths and weaknesses by discussing a few of your own. Tell how your own personal makeup has influenced your areas of ministry.

Show your students a jigsaw puzzle. Describe how each piece is different but essential to the whole picture, just as the kids in your group have different gifts and talents that, when added together, make a powerful Christian group.

Thinking through the questions

When the questionnaires are completed, match each student's strengths to areas of ministry in your church. For example, form the actors and comedians (question 10) into a stage troupe.

The weaknesses you uncover will help you tailor messages and personal time with kids so that these needs can be addressed. There are ten weaknesses dealt with here—that's enough for ten messages!

A HARD LOOK INSIDE

Name (optional) _____

Rate yourself in each of the following areas by circling the appropriate number. (1 = Weak, 10 = Strong)

1. My commitment to Christ is:
   1 2 3 4 5 6 7 8 9 10

2. My obedience to Christ and his Word is:
   1 2 3 4 5 6 7 8 9 10

3. My public example as a Christian is:
   1 2 3 4 5 6 7 8 9 10

4. My diligence in reading the Bible is:
   1 2 3 4 5 6 7 8 9 10

5. My willingness to serve the church is:
   1 2 3 4 5 6 7 8 9 10

6. My private moral life is:
   1 2 3 4 5 6 7 8 9 10

7. My integrity (honesty) is:
   1 2 3 4 5 6 7 8 9 10

8. My use of speech is:
   1 2 3 4 5 6 7 8 9 10

9. My knowledge of spiritual things is:
   1 2 3 4 5 6 7 8 9 10

10. My prayer life is:
    1 2 3 4 5 6 7 8 9 10

11. My involvement in the youth group is:
    1 2 3 4 5 6 7 8 9 10

12. My attendance at church is:
    1 2 3 4 5 6 7 8 9 10

13. My loyalty to this body of believers is:
    1 2 3 4 5 6 7 8 9 10

14. My desire to serve God with my life is:
    1 2 3 4 5 6 7 8 9 10

15. My sense of having a purposeful life is:
    1 2 3 4 5 6 7 8 9 10

16. My priorities, as compared with God's priorities, are:
    1 2 3 4 5 6 7 8 9 10

17. My willingness to be an example to new Christians is:
    1 2 3 4 5 6 7 8 9 10

18. My use of my talents and resources for Christ is:
    1 2 3 4 5 6 7 8 9 10

19. My love for those who are different or unlovely is:
    1 2 3 4 5 6 7 8 9 10

20. My willingness to avoid being part of a clique is:
    1 2 3 4 5 6 7 8 9 10

HOW TO USE
A Hard Look Inside

Use this questionnaire when you want your kids to focus on how well (or poorly) they live by the precepts of the Christian faith. It is serious in nature and should follow a challenge to excel in Christian living.

Keep in mind that some kids tend to score themselves artificially low, while others tend to exaggerate their achievements. Instead of comparing one response sheet to another, look to see how each individual perceives his or her strengths and weaknesses.

Suggested classroom activities
This questionnaire can be the trigger to build a prayer meeting. Each question raises an issue for which students can pray.

The questions touch on issues essential to a Christian's spiritual health. You can start the ball rolling by discussing how people maintain physical health (proper diet, proper exercise, and rest). Compare those steps to maintaining one's spiritual health.

Thinking through the questions
The questions fall into two categories: Those that deal with attitudes (questions 14, 15, 17, and others) and those that deal with actions (questions 4, 8, 11, and others). Both are equally important, but kids often think of the Christian life only in terms of behavior. It's a good idea to develop a series of messages that stress the importance of your group's inner qualities. Either way, you have twenty important topics from which to choose.

How I Use My Day

1. What time do you get up on school days?

   What time do you go to bed?

2. What time do you get up on weekend or vacation days?

   What time do you go to bed?

3. Write down the approximate number of hours you spend doing the following things during a typical school day (to the nearest half hour):

   ___ Sleeping   ___ Hanging out with friends
   ___ Homework   ___ Practicing music, dance, etc.
   ___ Devotions   ___ Travel
   ___ Phone calls   ___ Shopping
   ___ Chores   ___ Church activities
   ___ Family time   ___ Listening to music
   ___ School   ___ Reading
   ___ Job   ___ Watching TV, videos, movies
   ___ Eating   ___ Grooming (showering, dressing, etc.)
   ___ Sports   ___ Other

4. How many hours of free time do you have on a school day?

5. Write down the approximate number of hours you spend doing the following things during a typical weekend day or vacation day (to the nearest half hour):

   ___ Sleeping   ___ Hanging out with friends
   ___ Homework   ___ Practicing music, dance, etc.
   ___ Devotions   ___ Travel
   ___ Phone calls   ___ Shopping
   ___ Chores   ___ Church activities
   ___ Family time   ___ Listening to music
   ___ School   ___ Reading
   ___ Job   ___ Watching TV, videos, movies
   ___ Eating   ___ Grooming (showering, dressing, etc.)
   ___ Sports   ___ Other

6. How many hours of free time do you have on a weekend day or vacation day?

7. Which of the following statements seems most like you? (check one)

   ___ I never have enough time to do all the things that I want.
   ___ I feel I have a good balance between work, recreation, school and relaxation.
   ___ I am often bored and don't have much to do that is any fun.

8. If you had more free time, how would you spend it?

9. Do you spend any of your free time doing acts of service for the church, the youth group, poor people, missions, and so on?
   ___ Yes ___ No

10. How many of your waking hours are spent alone and quiet each day?

11. Would you consider time spent on video games as wasted time?
    ___ Yes ___ No

    Why or why not?

12. How would you rate your use of time? (check one)
    ___ I use my time profitably.
    ___ I sometimes get things done and sometimes waste time.
    ___ I spin my wheels a lot.

HOW TO USE
How I Use My Day

How do your students spend their hours? They will think this question through as they work on this questionnaire. They will have a chance to consider principles of good stewardship of time. An extra dividend is that the information will help you to schedule weekly events or plan a calendar of youth activities.

When ready to begin the questionnaire, tell students to make the closest guesses they can about exact times or amounts.

Suggested classroom activities

This questionnaire can begin a Bible study or lesson on time management, self-discipline, laziness, and other related topics.

A clock is a good visual aid when speaking of the importance of time. Read Eph. 5:15-16 also.

To conclude the class time, have students consider areas where they can reduce wasted time to make room for more devotional minutes.

Thinking through the questions

After students work on Questions 3 and 5, have them check to see that their days add up to about 24 hours. If they don't, either your kids are too busy or too undisciplined!

Question 8 is likely to be answered a bit dishonestly—students may want to believe they would do more good things, when in fact they might just watch more TV. Caution them to answer this question carefully and accurately.

Question 9 gives you an idea of who is active in Christian service and who needs a change in priorities.

Question 10 might have been answered differently a couple of generations ago. Quiet time can be a wonderful elixir, but few kids take advantage of it. Encourage your students to experiment with being alone and quiet with God.

Compare each student's answer to question 12 with the rest of his or her responses. Do they match up? If not, a message or two on what things are truly important in life, and what things are not, could be in order.

Self-discipline & Me

Check one answer to finish each statement.

1. Looking at myself:
___ I think that I have good self-control.
___ I have some trouble with self-control.
___ I have no self-control.

2. My ability to control myself:
___ is often affected by my moods or feelings.
___ is usually unaffected by my moods or feelings.

3. When I work on a project:
___ I almost always finish what I start.
___ I sometimes finish what I start.
___ I never finish what I start.

4. When I give my word:
___ I keep it.
___ I try to keep it.
___ I keep it if it's convenient.

5. When I say that I'll be someplace at a certain time:
___ I make a point of being prompt.
___ I'm usually a little late.
___ I often inconvenience others by being very late.

6. My behavior:
___ is seldom affected by my moods.
___ is occasionally affected by my moods.
___ is often affected by my moods.

7. When I find something challenging that I want to do:
___ I start planning and working towards that goal.
___ I daydream about what it would be like to do but rarely get around to it.

8. Around the house:
___ I accept responsibility for my share of the chores and do not need to be reminded to do them.
___ My parents have to remind me before I get any work done.
___ My parents have to nag and discipline me in order to get my help.

9. When it comes to honesty:
___ I tell the truth, even though it many be difficult at times.
___ I tell the truth unless it will hurt someone's feelings.
___ I tell the truth as long as it won't get me or one of my friends in trouble.
___ Let's face it, I'm basically dishonest.

HOW TO USE
Self-discipline & Me

Self-discipline is tough for many kids as well as quite a few adults. This simple evaluation will help your students see how well they are able to apply self-control and discipline to various areas of their lives.

Some kids might find the results of a survey like this to be discouraging. Make sure to point out that perfect self-discipline is a goal that is beyond the reach of anyone. Because we fail or fall short does not mean we should give up. Instead, we can work to grow in the areas of our shortcomings.

Suggested classroom activities

To kick off the class time, talk about the various ways a star athlete has to exercise discipline in order to become a champion (pick a sport your students enjoy). Point out that to live life successfully, a person has to apply principles of self-discipline.

To conclude the class time, you can create opportunities to help your kids strengthen their self-discipline muscles. This is best done by inches rather than miles. For example, if a student really wants to spend more time reading the Bible, a plan might be devised to read one or two short passages a day for a given period of time. If the young person is successful, he or she can reach for a higher level of commitment to Bible reading. This kind of plan is most helpful when there is another person acting as an encourager and coach.

Thinking through the questions

Questions 1 and 2 deal with self-control. What is the difference between self-control and self-discipline? Self-control means to exercise control over one's emotions, desires, and actions, while self-discipline speaks more of training oneself for the sake of development.

The rest of the questions focus on important areas of character (honesty, dependability, responsibility, and so on). A person who is doing well in these areas is mature. Challenge your students to consider what their answers tell them about their maturity level.

How I Treat My Parents

1. Do you often express gratitude for things your parents do and provide?
___ Yes ___ No ___ Sometimes

2. Do you apologize to or ask for forgiveness from your parents when you do or say something wrong?
___ Yes ___ No ___ Sometimes

3. Do you speak respectfully to your parents?
___ Yes ___ No ___ Sometimes

4. Are all areas of your life open to inspection?
___ Yes ___ No ___ Sometimes

5. Do you avoid tricking or deceiving your parents?
___ Yes ___ No ___ Sometimes

6. Do you keep your word to your parents?
___ Yes ___ No ___ Sometimes

7. Are you faithful in doing what your parents expect you to do?
___ Yes ___ No ___ Sometimes

8. Do you live a life your parents would be proud of?
___ Yes ___ No ___ Sometimes

9. Do you carry your fair share of household responsibilities without grumbling?
___ Yes ___ No ___ Sometimes

10. Do you occasionally ask your parents if there is anything you can do to help around the house?
___ Yes ___ No ___ Sometimes

11. Do you do nice things for your parents occasionally without any motive?
___ Yes ___ No ___ Sometimes

12. Do you put forth your best effort at school?
___ Yes ___ No ___ Sometimes

13. Do you listen to your parents when they share their advice or opinions?
___ Yes ___ No ___ Sometimes

14. Do you ask for your parents' advice about major decisions you have to make?
___ Yes ___ No ___ Sometimes

15. Do you try to put yourself in your parents' shoes when you and they don't see eye to eye?
___ Yes ___ No ___ Sometimes

16. Do you attempt to compromise with your parents rather than insist on having it your way?
___ Yes ___ No ___ Sometimes

17. Do you accept no for an answer without argument?
___ Yes ___ No ___ Sometimes

18. Do you try to keep peace at home with your brothers and sisters?
___ Yes ___ No ___ Sometimes

19. Do you treat your parents' possessions with care?
___ Yes ___ No ___ Sometimes

20. Do you return things that you borrow from your parents promptly and in good condition?
___ Yes ___ No ___ Sometimes

21. Do you accept responsibility if you foul up with your parents?
___ Yes ___ No ___ Sometimes

22. Do you demonstrate wisdom in the way you handle your money?
___ Yes ___ No ___ Sometimes

23. Do you make the most of the opportunities that your parents have provided you?
___ Yes ___ No ___ Sometimes

24. Do you ever ask your parents to pray with you?
___ Yes ___ No ___ Sometimes

25. Do you thank God for giving you the parents you have?
___ Yes ___ No ___ Sometimes

HOW TO USE
How I Treat My Parents

This questionnaire is designed as a reality check for students in how they relate to their parents. Kids may become a little more sensitive to problems they sometimes cause their parents.

Suggested classroom activities

This questionnaire can be used as part of a lesson or Bible study. It can be teamed with the *How I Treat My Kids* adult questionnaire as part of a parent-teen night. It can be given to adults as well as kids, comparing the results. Many of the questions can offer great stimulus for discussion.

Thinking through the questions

Questions 1-3 deal with the way kids talk to their parents. Words can build up or break down.

Questions 4-8 speak of honesty and trustworthiness.

Questions 9-12 help students check their laziness factor.

Questions 13 and 14 talk about seeking advice from a parent.

Questions 15-18 deal with arguments and how they can be handled or avoided.

Questions 19 and 20 revolve around how to treat another person's possessions.

The rest of the questions deal with various topics, including a spiritual focus in questions 24 and 25.

HOW I TREAT MY KIDS

1. Do you use the same kind of language that you expect your kids to use?
___ Yes ___ No ___ Sometimes

2. Do you avoid nagging or complaining to your kids?
___ Yes ___ No ___ Sometimes

3. Do you thank your kids when they do something for you?
___ Yes ___ No ___ Sometimes

4. Do you ridicule your kids' dress or taste in music?
___ Yes ___ No ___ Sometimes

5. Do you affirm or praise your kids for what they do right at least as much as you criticize them when they do wrong?
___ Yes ___ No ___ Sometimes

6. Do you control your temper?
___ Yes ___ No ___ Sometimes

7. Do you avoid venting anger or frustration from daily pressures on your kids?
___ Yes ___ No ___ Sometimes

8. Do you avoid judging or disciplining in haste or during the heat of the moment?
___ Yes ___ No ___ Sometimes

9. Do you attempt to speak with love about those who may cause you aggravation?
___ Yes ___ No ___ Sometimes

10. Do you openly show affection to your kids?
___ Yes ___ No ___ Sometimes

11. Do you treat all your children with equal fairness?
___ Yes ___ No ___ Sometimes

12. Do you avoid comparing your children negatively to others?
___ Yes ___ No ___ Sometimes

13. Do you treat your kids as if you trust them?
___ Yes ___ No ___ Sometimes

14. Do you apologize to your kids when you have done something wrong?
___ Yes ___ No ___ Sometimes

15. Do you make your kids' friends feel welcome and accepted in your home?
___ Yes ___ No ___ Sometimes

16. Do you listen carefully when your kids are talking to you?
___ Yes ___ No ___ Sometimes

17. Do you demonstrate honesty and truthfulness in front of your kids?
___ Yes ___ No ___ Sometimes

18. Do you keep your promises to your kids?
___ Yes ___ No ___ Sometimes

19. Do you demonstrate financial integrity and self-control in front of your kids?
___ Yes ___ No ___ Sometimes

20. Do you avoid habits and actions that you don't want your kids to imitate?
___ Yes ___ No ___ Sometimes

21. Do you allow your kids to experience the consequences of their mistakes without covering for them?
___ Yes ___ No ___ Sometimes

22. Do you avoid circumventing your spouse's authority or discipline with your kids?
___ Yes ___ No ___ Sometimes

23. Do you model a strong spiritual life in front of your kids?
___ Yes ___ No ___ Sometimes

24. Do you pray with your kids?
___ Yes ___ No ___ Sometimes

How I Treat My Kids

As a youth worker, you've learned that not all parents are great examples for their children to follow. This questionnaire is designed to alert parents to several important principles of good parenting—encouragement, affection, spiritual life, discipline, and others.

This questionnaire is best used when parents are gathered together to talk about relationships with their teens.

Suggested classroom activities
How I Treat My Kids can also be given to the kids (to be filled out from their perspectives) so you can contrast their perceptions with their parents' perceptions.

When working with the adults, provide resources such as books on parenting and family matters. A parenting seminar with a special speaker, such as *Understanding Your Teenager* with Wayne Rice, would be great. (For more information, call 619-561-9309.)

Thinking through the questions
Questions 1-5 focus on language—what do parents say to their children? Is there swearing, nagging, and ridicule or affirmation, praise, and appreciation?

Questions 6-9 speak of temper and aggravation. Every parent gets angry now and then, but anger must be handled properly (see Eph. 4:26-27).

Questions 10-16 deal with affection, acceptance, and trust.

Questions 17-20 center on a parent's demonstrations of honesty and self-control.

Question 22 raises an issue that can cause real problems in a family: discipline. It is very important that parents agree on how and when discipline should be applied. You may wish to have the name of one or two good family counselors on hand in case a parent expresses concern over this issue.

Questions 23 and 24 speak of the spiritual aspect of parenting. This is a good time to present the Gospel if you have unchurched parents in the room.

MY PERSONALITY

1. I smile a lot.
___ Yes ___ No

2. I like to laugh a lot.
___ Yes ___ No

3. People think of me as the class clown.
___ Yes ___ No

4. When people say hello, I'm quick to be friendly.
___ Yes ___ No

5. I'm shy.
___ Yes ___ No

6. If someone makes a joke at my expense, I almost never take offense.
___ Yes ___ No

7. I'm a good listener; people like to talk with me.
___ Yes ___ No

8. When I talk to people, I always remember and use their name.
___ Yes ___ No

9. People often ask me for advice.
___ Yes ___ No

10. When someone tells me something, I keep my mouth shut!
___ Yes ___ No

11. I'm a loyal person; I stick by my friends.
___ Yes ___ No

12. I see the importance of making people feel special and try to do that for others.
___ Yes ___ No

13. I encourage others:
___ Often ___ Sometimes ___ Almost never

14. I put people down.
___ Yes ___ No

15. I blame others for their mistakes.
___ Yes ___ No

16. I'm an interesting person.
___ Yes ___ No

17. I'm impulsive.
___ Yes ___ No

18. I've been known to flare up in anger.
___ Yes ___ No

19. I tend to brag:
___ Too much ___ Occasionally ___ Almost never

20. I work hard to reach my goals.
___ Yes ___ No

HOW TO USE
My Personality

A questionnaire on personality always generates student interest. We all are interested in how others perceive us. This questionnaire selects the most common areas in which a healthy personality manifests itself and it reveals the areas that can create friction with others. A church with kids who have healthy personalities has one key to an attractive and growing group!

There are three basic uses for this questionnaire: first, to make each of your kids aware of personality; second, to make you aware of how your kids perceive their own personalities; third, to give you a natural opening for lessons or Bible studies on the need for a healthy personality and how to develop it.

Suggested classroom activities
Talk about famous personalities and what makes them great. Have your students consider how the traits mentioned on the questionnaire point the way to a likable personality.

For a fun guessing game, shout out personality traits and have students choose the best examples of those traits from the group. These traits need to be positive—traits like funny, generous, friendly, encouraging, loyal, and so on. To avoid making anyone feel left out, stop the game after only a small fraction of the kids have been picked, or have student leaders and adults primed to call out the names of students who may usually be overlooked.

Thinking through the questions
The questions are divided into five areas of personality: humor, introversion and extroversion, listening, encouragement, and miscellaneous traits.

Questions 1-3 explore a person's "upbeat quotient." Kids are drawn to people who see the sunny side of things.

Questions 4-6 deal with introversion or extroversion. It is important that any group have both kinds of kids. Extroverts can be leaders and chargers; introverts can be grounded, dependable and deep. God uses both types to grow his church.

Questions 7-10 ask your students, "Are you a good listener?" Listening is an important way to make others feel valued and loved.

Questions 11-15 can identify students who know how to encourage and build up others. A group that excels at this will grow.

Questions 16-20 focus on miscellaneous but important personality traits.

What About the Church?

1. Which book in the Bible tells us most about the first church? (circle one)

   Genesis   Revelation   Acts   1 Corinthian   Isaiah   James

2. The first church was started in what city? (circle one)

   Rome   Galilee   Jordan   Bethlehem   Jerusalem   Jericho

3. The first church was made mostly of what group of people? (circle one)

   Roman   Jewish   Asian   European   Greek   Everyone

4. The first church was what denomination? (circle one)

   Baptist   Methodist   Presbyterian   Catholic   Lutheran   None

5. In which of the following was the first church started? (circle one)

   Committee room   Rally   Easter service   Prayer meeting

6. What is the best definition of "church?" (circle one)

   A building   A sacred place   A group of people   A meeting

7. Which one of the people below gave the first sermon in the first church? (circle one)

   John   Philip   Paul   Peter   David   Moses

8. When (approximately) did the first church begin? (circle one)

   1010 years ago   3050 years ago   650 years ago   2000 years ago

9. Which two people listed below were persecutors of the early church? (circle two)

   David   Saul   Goliath   Nero   Pilate   Pharaoh   Herod

10. Which one of the following is a common title for the church? (circle one)

    The Great Gathering   Those of the Truth   The Body of Christ

11. Within hours of its beginning, the first church had how many members? (circle one)

    Dozens   Hundreds   Thousands   Millions

12. Jesus preached often at the early church.

    ___ Yes ___ No

HOW TO USE
What About the Church?

Do your kids have a good understanding of the church—its meaning, purpose, and history? No! Well, almost certainly not. This questionnaire is designed to evaluate how well your group understands the church. It will show you what basics your students need to learn.

Suggested classroom activities
This is a good time to kick off a study on the book of Acts. Also, you may wish to emphasize the spiritual purpose of a local church. Beyond the fun aspects of a typical youth group, that group has a God-given reason to exist. Bible study, outreach, and discipleship and more are all aspects of your group's purpose. Discuss these with your kids.

Thinking through the questions
Question 1: Acts
Question 2: Jerusalem
Question 3: Jewish
Question 4: None (be prepared to explain why denominations exist)
Question 5: Prayer meeting (is your group built on prayer?)
Question 6: A group of people
Question 7: Peter
Question 8: 2000
Question 9: Saul and Nero (point out that Saul became Paul, a pivotal pioneer in Christianity)
Question 10: The body of Christ
Question 11: Thousands
Question 12: No (he ascended into heaven before the church was founded)

What About the Bible?

1. The Bible consists of how many books? (circle one)
   100   59   27   66   15

2. The Bible has two main divisions. What are they called? (circle one)
   Major and minor prophets   Past and future books
   Old and New Testaments

3. What books in the Bible tell about the life of Jesus Christ? (circle one)
   The Psalms   The Epistles   The Gospels
   The Prophesies   The Proverbs

4. What is the first book in the Bible? (circle one)
   Jonah   Genesis   Malachi
   1 Corinthians   Revelations

5. What is the last book in the Bible? (circle one)
   Revelation   Ephesians   1 John
   Malachi   Jude

6. What book contains the longest chapter in the Bible? (circle one)
   Matthew   Hezekiah   Revelation   Genesis   Psalms

7. Which book of the Bible listed below tells about God creating people? (circle one)
   Jude   Revelation   Jonah
   Ephesians   Genesis   Job

8. Who wrote the Bible? (circle one)
   Inspired men   Almighty God
   Monks and priests   Jesus   Who knows?

9. The New Testament has how many books? (circle one)
   34   56   27   18   44

10. The story of the birth of Jesus Christ is recorded in which of the following books? (circle one)
    Luke   Genesis   Acts   Romans   1 Corinthians

11. What is the last book of the Old Testament? (circle one)
    Zechariah   Malachi   Zephaniah   Romans   Galatians

12. Which book describes the beginning of the church? (circle one)
    Romans   Jude   Acts   John

The Bible can be intimidating, even to those who want to know more about it. This Bible trivia questionnaire can serve as an encouragement to those students who are committed to making the attempt.

Suggested classroom activities

There are several versions of Bible trivia games on the market; get and play one with your group. Give simple awards, such as fun certificates, to those who get the most questions right (or wrong).

Teach your students Bible study principles and what sort of reference work resources are available in your church library or Christian bookstore.

Thinking through the questions

Question 1: 66
Question 2: Old and New Testaments
Question 3: The Gospels
Question 4: Genesis
Question 5: Revelation
Question 6: Psalms (119)
Question 7: Genesis
Question 8: Inspired men
Question 9: 27
Question 10: Luke
Question 11: Malachi
Question 12: Acts

What About Jesus?

1. Circle the phrases that best describe Jesus to you.
   A great prophet   The greatest moral teacher
   The son of God   The Savior

2. On what holiday do we celebrate the resurrection of Jesus Christ? (circle one)
   Halloween   Thanksgiving   Easter
   Christmas   4th of July   Good Friday

3. In which book do we learn about the birth of Jesus Christ? (circle one)
   Ephesians   Romans   Luke   Genesis   Jonah   Acts

4. About how old was Jesus Christ when he died? (circle one)
   65   42   33   50   27

5. What race was Jesus? (circle one)
   European   Latin   Oriental   Greek   Jewish   African

6. Who betrayed Jesus? (circle one)
   Matthew   Paul   Nathaniel   Judas
   John   Barabbas   Pilate

7. What was the main reason the Jewish leaders hated Jesus? (circle one)
   He argued with them
   He claimed to be God
   He did miracles

8. Joseph taught Jesus what trade? (circle one)
   Fishing   Tentmaking   Carpentry
   Tax collecting   Plumbing

9. What was the most unusual thing about Jesus? (circle one)
   He healed the sick
   He rose from the dead
   He died on a cross

10. Jesus lived about how many years ago? (circle one)
    600 years ago   1000 years ago
    2000 years ago   3000 years ago

11. Which of the following people personally knew Jesus well? (circle all that apply)
    Job   Jonah   Paul   James   Apollo
    Enoch   John   Thomas   Timothy

12. What famous sermon did Jesus deliver? (circle one)
    The Sermon on the Mount
    The Sermon on the Lake
    The Sermon in the Temple

13. Which of the following are names and titles given to Jesus in the Bible? (circle all that apply)
    The Door   The Window   Emmanuel
    The Good Shepherd   The Bread of Health

HOW TO USE
What About Jesus?

What do your students know about the one they claim to follow? Find out with this questionnaire. It's not at all hard, so it might be a bit discouraging if your students fail miserably. (If you fail miserably, that's another story!)

Suggested classroom activities
After everyone has worked on the questionnaire, have someone play the part of Jesus answering the questions as they are asked at a first-century press conference. Your students play the reporters.

Thinking through the questions
Question 1: The Son of God and Savior
Question 2: Easter
Question 3: Luke
Question 4: 33
Question 5: Jewish
Question 6: Judas
Question 7: He claimed to be God
Question 8: Carpentry
Question 9: He rose from the dead
Question 10: 2000
Question 11: James, John, and Thomas
Question 12: The Sermon on the Mount
Question 13: The Door, Emmanuel, The Good Shepherd

I Wanna Know

What do you want to learn about in youth group? You can tell us by rating your interest in all the topics on this questionnaire.
(1 = not interested, 5 = strongly interested)

1. How the Bible became the Bible
1 2 3 4 5

2. The Bible book of Revelation and its prophecies about the future
1 2 3 4 5

3. Ethics: what's right and wrong—and how to tell
1 2 3 4 5

4. The who and how of dating
1 2 3 4 5

5. How to share Christ with my friends
1 2 3 4 5

6. Christian vocations such as pastor, youth director, missionary, and so on
1 2 3 4 5

7. Books of the Bible
1 2 3 4 5
Which ones?

8. How to understand my parents
1 2 3 4 5

9. How to become a Christian
1 2 3 4 5

10. How the church started and what it's all about
1 2 3 4 5

11. What cults believe
1 2 3 4 5

12. What other major religions believe
1 2 3 4 5

13. Christian love
1 2 3 4 5

14. Heaven and hell
1 2 3 4 5

15. Spiritual gifts: what they are and how to use them
1 2 3 4 5

16. How to wisely counsel my friends on tough subjects
1 2 3 4 5

17. Science and the teaching of the Bible
1 2 3 4 5

18. Gossip, slander, and the tongue
1 2 3 4 5

19. How to really study the Bible
1 2 3 4 5

20. What it means to be a disciple of Jesus Christ
1 2 3 4 5

21. Unity and genuine fellowship in the church
1 2 3 4 5

22. What the Bible really teaches about drugs and alcohol
1 2 3 4 5

23. What the Bible says about homosexuality
1 2 3 4 5

24. Abortion, war, gene alteration, and other current issues
1 2 3 4 5

25. What the Bible says about the stuff we listen to
1 2 3 4 5

26. How to use time more wisely
1 2 3 4 5

27. What the Bible says about getting wealthy and using my cash
1 2 3 4 5

28. What being and having a friend is all about
1 2 3 4 5

29. Why God allows bad things to happen to innocent people
1 2 3 4 5

30. How we can show love and be compassionate to those who are hard to love
1 2 3 4 5

HOW TO USE
I Wanna Know

I Wanna Know can be used to pack relevance into your curriculum. This questionnaire will tell you what your students want to learn about.

An especially good time to use this questionnaire is when a new group of kids graduate into your program.

Suggested classroom activities

If time allows, you can quickly tabulate the answers for all to see. On the chalkboard list the numbers 1 through 30. Have students raise their hands only for those that received high ratings (4s and 5s on the scale). Pick the ten highest-rated items as your future teaching subjects. If you like, have students then vote on which subjects from the Top Ten they want to study first.

Thinking through the questions

The themes covered by the questions include Bible knowledge, ethics, dating, Christian living, relationships with parents, spiritual gifts, and homosexuality. Those items that receive the strongest response are your topics for future group study.

LIAR, LIAR, PANTS ON FIRE

Circle one answer for each question.

1. If it would save me or a friend from big trouble, I would lie.

   This is okay   This is wrong   Sometimes it's okay

2. Ken's father consistently drives ten to fifteen miles per hour over the speed limit.

   This is okay   This is wrong   Sometimes it's okay

3. Fallon's father is a police officer. Off duty, he drives ten to fifteen miles per hour over the speed limit.

   This is okay   This is wrong   Sometimes it's okay

4. To keep her little boy quiet in the grocery store, Bob's mom gives him grapes to eat before she's had them weighed and paid for.

   This is okay   This is wrong   Sometimes it's okay

5. Ben copies a friend's CD.

   This is okay   This is wrong   Sometimes it's okay

6. Coin collector Jeff gives a little kid a dime for a penny Jeff knows is worth about $200.

   This is okay   This is wrong   Sometimes it's okay

7. Sheldon always dumps his car's used oil in the back yard.

   This is okay   This is wrong   Sometimes it's okay

8. Doug works at a gas station. He takes a wrench home to work on his car. He keeps it.

   This is okay   This is wrong   Sometimes it's okay

9. Ron asks Sue for a date. Sue has nothing to do, but is hoping Dan will call her. To avoid hurting Ron's feelings, she tells him she has to baby-sit.

   This is okay   This is wrong   Sometimes it's okay

10. Sara needs a good grade in English. Her book report is due soon. Bill agrees to do her report for $20.

    This is okay   This is wrong   Sometimes it's okay

11. Rosalie thinks God probably wants her to put her five dollars in the collection plate, but she decides to buy lunch.

    This is okay   This is wrong   Sometimes it's okay

12. Shaun and Brenda make the perfect couple. Since they intend to marry, they engage in sexual activity.

    This is okay   This is wrong   Sometimes it's okay

13. Angie passes on a "juicy tidbit" about Harmony. Everybody is going to hear about it anyway, Angie thinks, so there's no problem with passing it on.

    This is okay   This is wrong   Sometimes it's okay

14. Harmony is offended by Angie's gossip; the friendship is broken.

    This is okay   This is wrong   Sometimes it's okay

Liar, Liar, Pants on Fire

What is right and wrong? Should I follow the crowd? Why should I do this and not that? It's not easy to grow from a child to an adult; a teenager needs help and guidance. The answers to this questionnaire will reveal many of the issues and controversies your students face.

As a youth worker, you can have a tremendous impact on your students' thinking and behavior. Use this questionnaire to help you choose which areas require your attention.

Suggested classroom activities

Introduce this questionnaire by saying something like, "When we talk about ethics we talk about things like truth or lies, honesty or cheating, obedience or disobedience, right or wrong. Your views on what is right and what is wrong will affect your entire life. That's why we want to get into the issue of ethics now. It's important that we learn the difference between right and wrong."

Another way to introduce the questionnaire is to ask students to define ethics and discuss why learning ethics is important.

To use this survey to your best advantage, try to anticipate the responses. Create questions to open more cans of worms. Review the suggested Scripture, preparing short talks based on each.

After the kids have filled out the questionnaire, let them keep their sheets in front of them. Then discuss their answers to each question. Close the discussion of each issue with the basic Biblical view on the ethic involved.

Thinking through the questions

The subjects covered are listed here with Scripture references to help you.

Questions 1 and 9: Lying (Ephesians 4:25)

Questions 2,3 and 5: Lawbreaking (1 Peter 2:13, 14)

Questions 4 and 8: Stealing (Ephesians 4:28)

Questions 6 and 10: Cheating (1 Corinthians 6:8)

Question 7 and 11: Stewardship (1 Corinthians 4:2)

Question 12: Sex (Romans 13:13, Ephesians 5:3)

Question 13: Gossip (Proverbs 11:13)

Question 14: Unforgiveness (Matthew 6:14,15)

END OF THE YEAR
Wrap-up

Age ____ Male ____ Female ____ Grade ____

1. How long have you attended our youth group activities? (circle one)

   A year or less   1-2 years   More than 2 years

2. What have you discovered about God this year?

3. You attend worship service at our church: (circle one)

   Regularly   Fairly often   Sometimes   Not often

   If you circled "Sometimes" or "Not often," let us know why you do not attend on a regular basis.

4. What activities this year did you enjoy the most?

5. What events or programs would you like to see us do next year?

6. What topics or subjects would you like us to discuss or teach during the coming year?

7. Would you like to be more involved in the life of the church or youth group in the coming year?

   ___ Yes ___ No

8. Would you like a chance to teach or speak in front of other kids?

   ___ Yes ___ No

9. If you had a problem, which of our staff people would you probably talk with?

10. Name two or three kids in the youth group who seem to be good examples of what a Christian should be like.

    1.

    2.

    3.

11. On the back of this paper, please write any suggestions you think would improve our church or youth group in the year to come. *Thanks!*

HOW TO USE
End of the Year Wrap-up

The end of the year is a perfect time to evaluate everything that has taken place. This kind of evaluation shows you what you have been doing right and what needs improvement. Invite your students to express their thoughts of praise and criticism.

Suggested classroom activities
This questionnaire can be helpful in launching a planning meeting. The questions will help your students think about what events worked well in the past and what jobs they might like to volunteer for.

Thinking through the questions
Question 2 gives valuable insight into the spiritual development of your group.

Question 3 identifies problem areas in your church's program.

Question 4 can tell you what you did that was a winner.

Questions 5 and 6 tell you what events to plan and what subjects to tackle.

Pay attention to question 10. Note the names given here, especially if they are repeated. These are the kids to encourage in leadership roles. Let them know that others look up to them.

Question 11 should be taken seriously. See what you can do to implement the ideas offered.

GUYS' PERSPECTIVE

Age _____ Grade _____

1. Would you feel weird if a girl asked you out?
    ___ Yes ___ No

2. If a girl invited you out, would you feel obligated to pay at least half of the tab?
    ___ Yes ___ No

3. Would you marry a girl who had a nice personality but was not physically attractive?
    ___ Yes ___ No

4. Would you marry an overweight girl?
    ___ Yes ___ No

5. Which is the best gift to buy a girl you like? (check one)
    ___ Clothes   ___ Inexpensive jewelry
    ___ Flowers   ___ Tape or CD
    ___ Stuffed Animal   ___ Perfume
    ___ Book   ___ Other:

6. Would you marry a girl who has herpes?
    ___ Yes ___ No

7. Would you be willing to marry a girl who has a history of sleeping around, but who has changed her behavior?
    ___ Yes ___ No

8. Which kind of girl most appeals to you? (check one)
    ___ Rugged and physical   ___ Quiet and mysterious
    ___ Very feminine   ___ The-girl-next-door type
    ___ Energetic and talkative ___ Quiet and mysterious

9. Would you want your future wife to have breast implants to make her bust larger?
    ___ Yes ___ No

10. Do you think most girls are not interested in guys who don't drive?
    ___ Yes ___ No

11. Which three of the following characteristics do you think most attract girls to guys? (check three)
    ___ Lots of money   ___ Romantic nature
    ___ Power   ___ Hard working
    ___ Fame and popularity ___ Integrity
    ___ Brains   ___ Strong body
    ___ Good looks   ___ Take-charge personality
    ___ Spiritual maturity   ___ Holds a good job
    ___ Sensitivity   ___ Likes children

12. Would you marry a girl you knew could not have children?
    ___ Yes ___ No

13. Which of the following do you think girls like the most? (check three)
    ___ Flowers
    ___ Love letters
    ___ Chances to talk together
    ___ Small gifts
    ___ Long romantic walks
    ___ Going out to dinner
    ___ Regular phone calls
    ___ Going shopping together
    ___ Hanging out together

14. If a guy puts a lot of money, thought and effort into a date, should he be rewarded with a kiss?
    ___ Yes ___ No

15. Girls want to be treated with courtesy and chivalry from guys they like.
    ___ Yes ___ No

16. Would you brag to your friends about your sexual adventures?
    ___ Yes ___ No

HOW TO USE
Guys' Perspective

This questionnaire is best used in conjunction with *Girls' Perspective, Guys Would Say . . .*, and *Girls Would Say . . .*, as explained below. By using these four questionnaires together, your boys and girls can discover how the other sex thinks and feels.

Guys' Perspective asks your male students to reveal attitudes, preferences, and stereotypes they have about girls. You will be able to assess their maturity levels in these areas so that you can help them grow.

WARNING: Many of these questions touch on sensitive areas. They're designed to elicit honest, rather than ideal, answers. Nonetheless, it's likely that they'll generate a lot of emotion and controversy. Be prepared for this, and be prepared to present the biblical perspectives on men, women, and what makes for healthy, God-honoring relationships.

Suggested classroom activities

Give copies of *Guys' Perspective* to your guys and *Girls' Perspective* to your girls. Collect the questionnaires and tally the results secretly while the guys work on *Girls Would Say . . .* and the girls work on *Guys Would Say . . .*.

When everyone is finished, tally the answers to the second set of questionnaires and compare them to the previous tally. This should be a lot of fun for your students—and produce some real fireworks!

Tallying the questionnaires can take time, especially for a big group. Enlist a number of adults to help you. Give each adult a few questionnaires to tally; then add the tallies together to get your final results.

Thinking through the questions

These four questionnaires are without a doubt the most controversial in this book. There is a fine line between eliciting and exposing the honest, actual attitudes guys and girls have toward one another and reinforcing hurtful stereotypes and disrespectful prejudices. Be prepared to share God's perspective on how men and women should view and treat one another as noted before, and be quick to cut off arguments or humor that could be devastating to individual students.

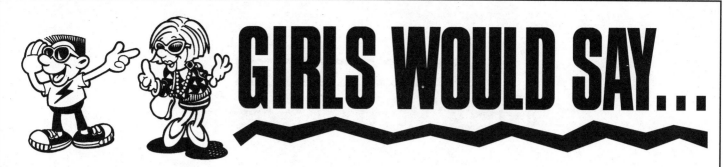

GIRLS WOULD SAY...

Guys, how well do you know the female mind? Indicate how you think the average girl would respond to the following questions.

1. The typical girl would go out with a guy she had no real feelings for if he took her somewhere she really wanted to go.
___ Yes ___ No

2. Would the average girl marry a guy who could not give her children?
___ Yes ___ No

3. Would the typical girl marry a guy who did not want children?
___ Yes ___ No

4. Would the typical girl marry a guy who had a low-paying job and little hope for future success?
___ Yes ___ No

5. In which areas do you think girls feel they should be absolutely equal with men? (check as many as apply)
___ Business ___ Politics
___ Military service ___ Physically demanding jobs
___ Roles in marriage ___ Job pay
___ Church leadership

6. Which gift do girls think a guy would most want to receive? (circle one)
Flowers Clothes Tape or CD Book Tools Cologne

7. Would a girl go out again with a guy who was physically aggressive on their first date, but stopped when asked to?
___ Yes ___ No

8. Would a girl marry a guy knowing he had herpes?
___ Yes ___ No

9. Would a girl marry a guy who dumped his fiancée or wife for her?
___ Yes ___ No

10. Do girls usually let others read the love letters they receive?
___ Yes ___ No

11. Which kind of guy do you think girls find most attractive? (check one)
___ Athletic ___ Artistic
___ Humorous ___ Quiet
___ Tough ___ Brainy
___ Sensitive ___ Romantic
___ Slick dresser ___ Good conversationalist

12. Would a girl marry a guy who wanted her to have breast implants?
___ Yes ___ No

13. Girls think a guy with a nice car is more attractive than a guy without one.
___ Yes ___ No

14. The typical girl would marry a guy 20 years older if he was in good shape, kind, and financially secure.
___ Yes ___ No

15. Which things do girls most want in their future husbands? (check three)
___ Leadership ___ Sensitivity
___ Power ___ Integrity
___ Courage ___ Romance
___ Brains ___ Lots of money
___ Spiritual maturity ___ Good job
___ Hard working ___ Likes children
___ Fame and popularity ___ Good looking

16. Girls think most guys would bail out or insist on an abortion if their girlfriend got pregnant.
___ Yes ___ No

17. Girls think guys most dislike: (check one)
___ Long phone conversations
___ Clothes shopping with his girlfriend
___ Dealing with a crying girlfriend
___ Hanging out with his girlfriend while his friends are doing something fun
___ Sharing his deeper feelings with his girlfriend

HOW TO USE
Girls Would Say...

This questionnaire is best used in conjunction with *Guys' Perspective*, *Girls' Perspective*, and *Guys Would Say . . .*, as explained below. By using these four questionnaires, your boys and girls can discover how the other sex thinks and feels.

Girls Would Say . . . asks your male students to tell what they think are the girls' attitudes, preferences, and stereotypes about guys. This is a lot of fun; your kids should have a great time.

WARNING: Many of these questions touch on sensitive areas. They're designed to elicit honest, rather than ideal, answers. Nonetheless, it's likely that they'll generate a lot of emotion and controversy. Be prepared for this, and be prepared to present the biblical perspectives on men, women, and what makes for healthy, God-honoring relationships.

Suggested classroom activities
Give copies of *Guys' Perspective* to your guys and *Girls' Perspective* to your girls. Collect the questionnaires and tally the results secretly while the guys work on *Girls Would Say . . .* and the girls work on *Guys Would Say . . .*.

When everyone is finished, tally the answers to the second set of questionnaires and compare them to the previous tally. This should be a lot of fun for your students—and produce some real fireworks!

Tallying the questionnaires can take time, especially for a big group. Enlist a number of adults to help you. Give each adult a few questionnaires to tally; then add the tallies together to get your final results.

Thinking through the questions
Girls Would Say . . . challenges your boys to read girls' minds—and face their lack of understanding about how girls really think. The difference in perceptions between the boys and girls makes a great staging point for discussion. For example, what if your boys think girls are not interested in church leadership (question 3) while your girls answer that they are strongly interested? Your group can gain insight into the real thoughts and feelings of the two sexes, and explore ways to bridge the often-yawning communication gap between men and women.

GIRLS' PERSPECTIVE

Age _____ Grade _____

1. Would you go out with a guy you had no feelings for if he took you somewhere you really wanted to go?
___ Yes ___ No

2. Would you marry a guy who could not give you children?
___ Yes ___ No

3. Would you marry a guy who did not want children?
___ Yes ___ No

4. Would you marry a guy with a low-paying job?
___ Yes ___ No

5. In which areas do you think women should be absolutely equal with men? (check as many as apply)
___ Business   ___ Politics
___ Military service   ___ Physically demanding jobs
___ Roles in marriage   ___ Job pay
___ Church leadership

6. Which of these things is the best gift to give a guy you like? (circle one)
Flowers   Clothes   Tape or CD   Book   Tools   Cologne

7. A guy you like becomes physically aggressive on your first date, but he stops when you insist. Would you date him again?
___ Yes ___ No

8. Would you marry a guy who had herpes?
___ Yes ___ No

9. Would you marry a guy who dumped his wife or fiancée for you?
___ Yes ___ No

10. Do you think the average girl lets others read the love letters she gets?
___ Yes ___ No

11. Which type of guy do girls find most attractive? (check one)
___ Athletic   ___ Artistic
___ Humorous   ___ Quiet
___ Tough   ___ Brainy
___ Sensitive   ___ Romantic
___ Slick dresser   ___ Good conversationalist
___ The-guy-next-door type

12. Would you marry a guy who wanted you to have breast implants?
___ Yes ___ No

13. Does the kind of a car a guy drives make any difference to the average girl?
___ Yes ___ No

14. Would you marry a guy 20 years older than you if he was in good shape, kind, and financially secure?
___ Yes ___ No

15. Which qualities or assets would you most want in a future husband? (check three)
___ Leadership   ___ Sensitivity
___ Power   ___ Integrity
___ Courage   ___ Romance
___ Brains   ___ Lots of money
___ Spiritual maturity   ___ Good job
___ Hard working   ___ Likes children
___ Fame and popularity   ___ Good looking

16. Would the average guy bail out or insist on an abortion if his girlfriend got pregnant?
___ Yes ___ No

17. Which of the following do guys dislike the most? (check one)
___ Long phone conversations
___ Clothes shopping with his girlfriend
___ Dealing with a crying girlfriend
___ Hanging out with his girlfriend while his friends are doing something fun
___ Sharing his deeper feelings with his girlfriend

HOW TO USE
Girls' Perspective

This questionnaire is best used in conjunction with *Guys' Perspective, Girls Would Say . . .*, and *Guys Would Say . . .*, as explained below. By using these four questionnaires, your boys and girls can discover how the other sex thinks and feels.

Girls' Perspective asks your female students to reveal attitudes, preferences, and stereotypes they have about guys. You will be able to assess their maturity level in these areas so that you can help them grow.

WARNING: Many of these questions touch on sensitive areas. They're designed to elicit honest, rather than ideal, answers. Nonetheless, it's likely that they'll generate a lot of emotion and controversy. Be prepared for this, and be prepared to present the biblical perspectives on men, women, and what makes for healthy, God-honoring relationships.

Suggested classroom activities

Give copies of *Guys' Perspective* to your guys and *Girls' Perspective* to your girls. Collect the questionnaires and tally the results secretly while the boys work on *Girls Would Say . . .* and the girls work on *Guys Would Say . . .*.

When everyone is finished, tally the answers to the second set of questionnaires and compare them to the previous tally. This should be a lot of fun for your students—and produce some real fireworks!

Tallying the questionnaires can take time, especially for a big group. Enlist a number of adults to help you. Give each adult a few questionnaires to tally; then add the tallies together to get your final results.

Thinking through the questions

These four questionnaires are without a doubt the most controversial in this book. There is a fine line between eliciting and exposing the honest, actual attitudes guys and girls have toward one another and reinforcing hurtful stereotypes and disrespectful prejudices. Be prepared to share God's perspective on how men and women should view and treat one another as noted before, and be quick to cut off arguments or humor that could be devastating to individual students.

GUYS WOULD SAY...

Girls, how well do you know the male mind? Indicate how you think the average guy would respond to the following questions.

1. Would an average guy tend to feel weird being asked out by a girl?
   ___ Yes ___ No

2. A guy who went out with a girl who invited him would still feel obligated to pay at least half of the tab.
   ___ Yes ___ No

3. The average guy would be interested in marrying a girl with a great personality but who is not physically attractive.
   ___ Yes ___ No

4. A guy would marry an overweight girl.
   ___ Yes ___ No

5. Which gift would a guy most likely think a girl would want? (check one)
   ___ Clothes   ___ Inexpensive jewelry
   ___ Flowers   ___ Tape or CD
   ___ Stuffed animal   ___ Perfume
   ___ Book   ___ Other:

6. The average guy would marry a girl with herpes.
   ___ Yes ___ No

7. The average guy would marry a girl who has a history of sleeping around, but who has changed her behavior.
   ___ Yes ___ No

8. Which kind of girl most appeals to the average guy? (check one)
   ___ Rugged and physical   ___ Quiet and mysterious
   ___ Very feminine   ___ The-girl-next-door type
   ___ Energetic and talkative ___ Career-oriented

9. A guy would want his wife to have breast implants to make her bust larger.
   ___ Yes ___ No

10. Guys think girls are not interested in them if they do not drive.
    ___ Yes ___ No

11. Guys think that girls are most attracted to which of the following characteristics? (check three)
    ___ Lots of money   ___ Romantic nature
    ___ Power   ___ Hard working
    ___ Fame and popularity ___ Integrity
    ___ Brains   ___ Strong body
    ___ Good looks   ___ Take-charge personality
    ___ Spiritual maturity ___ Good job
    ___ Sensitivity   ___ Likes kids

12. Would a guy marry a girl that he knew could not have children?
    ___ Yes ___ No

13. Which of the following items do guys think girls like the most?
    ___ Flowers   ___ Going out to dinner
    ___ Love letters   ___ Regular phone calls
    ___ Chances to talk together ___ Small gifts
    ___ Going shopping together ___ Long romantic walks
    ___ Hanging out together

14. The average guy expects a kiss if he puts a lot of money, thought, and effort into a date.
    ___ Yes ___ No

15. Guys think girls want to be treated with courtesy and chivalry by guys they like.
    ___ Yes ___ No

16. Do guys brag to each other about their sexual adventures?
    ___ Yes ___ No

HOW TO USE
Guys Would Say...

This questionnaire is best used in conjunction with *Guys' Perspective, Girls Would Say...*, and *Girls' Perspective*, as explained below. By using these four questionnaires, your boys and girls can discover how the other sex thinks and feels.

Guys Would Say... asks your female students to tell what they think are guys' attitudes, preferences, and stereotypes about girls. This is a lot of fun; your kids should have a great time.

WARNING: Many of these questions touch on sensitive areas. They're designed to elicit honest, rather than ideal, answers. Nonetheless, it's likely that they'll generate a lot of emotion and controversy. Be prepared for this, and be prepared to present the biblical perspectives on men, women, and what makes for healthy, God-honoring relationships.

Suggested classroom activities
Give copies of *Guys' Perspective* to your guys and *Girls' Perspective* to your girls. Collect the questionnaires and tally the results secretly while the guys work on *Girls Would Say...* and the girls work on *Guys Would Say....*

When everyone is finished, tally the answers to the second set of questionnaires and compare them to the previous tally. This should be a lot of fun for your students—and produce some real fireworks!

Tallying the questionnaires can take time, especially for a big group. Enlist a number of adults to help you. Give each adult a few questionnaires to tally; then add the tallies together to get your final results.

Thinking through the questions
Guys Would Say... challenges your girls to read the boys' minds—and face their lack of understanding about how guys really think. The difference in perceptions between girls and boys makes a great staging point for discussion. For example, do girls think boys are only interested in good-looking girls (question 3), while the boys indicate a high regard for personality? Your group will gain insight into the real thoughts and feelings of the two sexes, and explore how to bridge the often-yawning communication gap between men and women.

What I Could Do with My Summer Vacation

Summer vacation is a great time to do all sorts of things. Look over the list of things to do this summer and categorize the items using the following choices:

A - Absolutely!
B - Bright idea; I'll think about it
C - Can't decide
D - Don't think so
E - Ech!

___ 1. Mow someone's lawn for the love of Jesus, not money

___ 2. Write letters to relatives I don't see much

___ 3. Be part of a summer missions project

___ 4. Collect food, money, or goods for those who are needy

___ 5. Wash and wax my parents' car without being asked

___ 6. Teach a neighborhood kid how to ride a bike

___ 7. Hang out with the family rather than going off with friends

___ 8. Bring home a video that I know my brothers and sisters would enjoy more than me

___ 9. Work at a homeless shelter

___ 10. Work to earn money for missions, the poor, or the church

___ 11. Clean, repair, or refurbish some part of the church

___ 12. Make and serve my folks breakfast in bed

___ 13. Send thank-you notes to people who have been kind or caring to me

___ 14. Spend a week reading the Bible and other Christian books rather than watching TV

___ 15. Organize a birthday party for someone

___ 16. Take my parents to a play, concert, or movie they would enjoy

___ 17. Cook a meal for my minister or youth worker

___ 18. Throw an appreciation party for an unsung or overworked volunteer in the church

___ 19. Invite little kids in the neighborhood to come to Sunday school with my family

___ 20. Visit kids from an underprivileged area

___ 21. Go on vacation with my parents

HOW TO USE
What I Could Do with My Summer Vacation

This questionnaire is designed to stimulate your students' thinking about Christian service, the use of their time, and their willingness to be used by God. It is best used during spring or at the onset of summer, perhaps tied in with a challenge to participate in missions or service projects.

Suggested classroom activities

This questionnaire works very well at the end of a message, lesson, or Bible study on servanthood. The practical ideas or suggestions showing what could be done can be just the start of a large list that students could brainstorm together.

If you plan to use this questionnaire to motivate kids to serve in some kind of summer project, have the details of your project ready to present after this questionnaire has been completed.

Thinking through the questions

All the questions deal with things that young people can do to serve God by serving people. Some are simple, like mowing lawns and writing letters to relatives. You can tell your students that these are the sort of good things they could be doing all the time. Some of the projects, such as 3, 4, 9, and 10, require a greater commitment to fulfill. It may be good to encourage students to work in groups to accomplish these goals.

SPIRITUAL GIFT INVENTORY

Rate yourself in each of the following areas by circling the appropriate number.
- 1 = you are not gifted in that area
- 5 = you are strongly gifted in that area

1. God has inspired me to deliver one or more messages from him.
1 2 3 4 5

2. God has used me to lead and guide other believers.
1 2 3 4 5

3. I'm good at communicating information that helps others grow spiritually.
1 2 3 4 5

4. I'm good at discovering spiritual truths and can explain those truths to people.
1 2 3 4 5

5. The Holy Spirit gives me special insights.
1 2 3 4 5

6. People come to me for words of comfort, affirmation, and counsel.
1 2 3 4 5

7. I find it easy to know whether something is of God or of the devil.
1 2 3 4 5

8. I love to provide money and other resources for church work and other needs.
1 2 3 4 5

9. I'm good at helping get things done.
1 2 3 4 5

10. I show compassion and caring for others.
1 2 3 4 5

11. I have a strong desire to take the Gospel to other people, places, and cultures.
1 2 3 4 5

12. I find it easy to tell people about Jesus Christ.
1 2 3 4 5

13. I'm forever opening my home to use for Bible studies and other youth group activities.
1 2 3 4 5

14. I have confidence in God's ability to do great things.
1 2 3 4 5

15. When something needs to get done, people often look to me to take charge.
1 2 3 4 5

16. I love to plan the best way to reach goals.
1 2 3 4 5

17. God has done some pretty miraculous things through me.
1 2 3 4 5

18. I've prayed for people to be healed—and sometimes they have been!
1 2 3 4 5

19. I can speak in tongues.
1 2 3 4 5

20. I can interpret tongues.
1 2 3 4 5

21. To serve God without hindrance, it is my true desire to remain single forever.
1 2 3 4 5

22. People depend on me to do various jobs in the church and youth group.
1 2 3 4 5

HOW TO USE
Spiritual Gifts Inventory

This questionnaire is drawn from the Bible. It is designed to help kids get an inkling of which spiritual gifts they possess. The questions are hardly exhaustive; this is not a full-fledged gifts assessment program. However, each question will give you an opportunity to discuss a spiritual gift that some of your students may actually possess.

Suggested classroom activities
It remains up to you to provide ways your students can exercise their gifts. Give kids ideas on how they could put their gifts to work for the cause of Christ. Have your kids brainstorm ways that each gift could be used in your group and community.

Thinking through the questions
The gifts on the questionnaire are listed below:

Question 1: Prophecy (Romans 12:6; 1 Corinthians 12:10, 28)
Question 2: Pastor (Ephesians 4:11)
Question 3: Teaching (Romans 12:7; Ephesians 4:11; 1 Corinthians 12:28)
Question 4: Wisdom (1 Corinthians 12:8)
Question 5: Knowledge (1 Corinthians 12:8)
Question 6: Encouragement (Romans 12:8)
Question 7: Discerning of spirits (1 Corinthians 12:10)
Question 8: Giving (Romans 12:8)
Question 9: Helps (1 Corinthians 12:28)
Question 10: Mercy (Romans 12:8)
Question 11: Missionary (1 Corinthians 12:28; Ephesians 4:11)
Question 12: Evangelist (Ephesians 4:11)
Question 13: Hospitality (1 Peter 4:9, 10)
Question 14: Faith (1 Corinthians 12:9)
Question 15: Leadership (Romans 12:8)
Question 16: Administration (1 Corinthians 12:28)
Question 17: Miracles (1 Corinthians 12:10, 28)
Question 18: Healing (1 Corinthians 12:9, 28)
Question 19: Tongues (1 Corinthians 12:10, 28)
Question 20: Interpretation of tongues (1 Corinthians 12:10)
Question 21: Celibacy (Matthew 19:3-12)
Question 22: Service (Romans 12:7; 1 Peter 4:11)

Your Opinion, Please!

Age ____ Male ____ Female ____

1. Do you attend church, synagogue, or other religious services on a regular basis?
   ___ Yes ___ No

2. Do you believe that God exists?
   ___ Yes ___ No

3. Check the one statement that comes closest to your thoughts about God.
   ___ The idea of God is a fantasy.
   ___ God is real, but he is not involved in the lives of human beings.
   ___ God is like a force, not a personality.
   ___ God has a personality and can be pleased or displeased.
   ___ God cannot be known by human beings.

4. Circle the answer below that describes a human's basic inner nature.
   Good   Evil   Both   Neither

5. Do you believe there is eternal punishment for people like Hitler and Stalin?
   ___ Yes ___ No ___ Maybe

6. Do you believe in hell?
   ___ Yes ___ No

7. How would you define what it is to be a Christian? (check all that apply)
   ___ To be born in a Christian family
   ___ To go to a Christian church
   ___ To be a kind or good person
   ___ To believe that God actually exists
   ___ To be born again
   ___ To have a personal relationship with Jesus Christ
   ___ To have Jesus as your master and Lord
   ___ Other:

8. Do you think the Bible is the Word of God?
   ___ Yes ___ No

9. Do you believe that there is a place called heaven?
   ___ Yes ___ No

10. Do you believe that all religions are good and end up leading to the same place?
    ___ Yes ___ No

11. Have you ever read the New Testament?
    ___ Yes ___ No ___ Partially

12. Do you know any Christians that you respect for their sincere faith and actions?
    ___ Yes ___ No

13. How do you think of Jesus? (check all that apply)
    ___ Good man
    ___ Myth
    ___ Gifted teacher
    ___ Great prophet
    ___ Savior
    ___ Son of God

15. Do you think Christians should go around trying to convert other people?
    ___ Yes ___ No
    Why or why not?

HOW TO USE
Your Opinion, Please!

This questionnaire is designed to be taken to the public—out on the street, down at the beach, or over in the mall. It inquires about a person's beliefs—what he or she thinks about God and Christianity. Your kids can conduct this survey themselves.

Suggested classroom activities

Although *Your Opinion, Please!* is not intended for the classroom as the other questionnaires are, your students can conduct the survey themselves, then meet back to tally and discuss the results of the survey.

You can also use this questionnaire as a tool to share the Christian faith. Offer those who complete the questionnaire a Bible (or Bible portion) to take with them. Some may wish to discuss the questions. Make sure your kids have a decent grasp of how to explain their faith. This can be a low-key, informative, and effective way to take the truth to where people are.

Thinking through the questions

Here are a few Scripture passages that might come in handy when conducting the survey:

Question 1 discusses regular church attendance. See Hebrews 10:25. The existence of God (Question 2) is discussed in Hebrews 11:6. Question 3 (God's nature) lists various options, including the fact that God has personality. See Psalm 86:5 as one of many examples of God's personal nature. In the same vein, see Matthew 11:27, John 17:3, and Ephesians 1:17 to show that God can be known by human beings. Refer to Jeremiah 17:9 to see the evil nature of the heart (question 4). Hell is real, according to Revelation 20:10, 15 (questions 5 and 6). Some verses to use with question 7 are John 1:12; 3:3, 16; Revelation 3:20. Try 2 Timothy 3:16 and Hebrews 4:12 for question 8. Heaven (question 9) is discussed in many passages, including Matthew 4:17; 5:12; 6:1, 20; 2 Corinthians 5:1 and Philippians 3:20—pick your favorites. Only Christianity points the way to eternal life (question 10)—read John 14:6 and Acts 4:12. Examples of verses that can be used for question 13 are Matthew 26:63-64 and Romans 1:4. In the Great Commission (Matthew 29:19-20), we are commanded to share our faith (question 14).

THE EASTER QUIZ

1. Jesus met with his disciples for the last supper on the night of which Jewish holiday? (circle one)
   Yom Kippur   Hanukkah   Passover   Bar Mitzvah   Jubilee

2. Judas agreed to betray Jesus for how much money? (check one)
   ___ 40 pieces of silver   ___ 20 pieces of silver
   ___ 30 pieces of silver   ___ 50 pieces of eight

3. What did Judas do with the money? (circle one)
   ___ Threw it on the temple floor   ___ Bought a rope
   ___ Invested in real estate   ___ Gave it back
   ___ Gave it to the poor

4. Jesus was arrested by Roman soldiers.
   ___ Yes ___ No

5. Who beat Jesus? (circle one)
   Roman soldier   The public
   Jewish guards   Roman and Jewish guards

6. Who advised Pilate not to condemn Jesus? (circle one)
   His astrologers   His generals   His wife
   His guards   His friends

7. The Roman guards knelt down in front of Jesus, worshiping him as a king.
   ___ Yes ___ No

8. Pilate offered to release either Jesus or which criminal?
   Barnabas   Baal   Barabbas   Belshazzar

9. After the weakened Jesus could no longer carry his cross beam, who was forced to finish carrying it to the crucifixion site? (circle one)
   Simon   Caiaphas   Nicodemus   Lazarus

10. Jesus was crucified at Golgotha (Aramaic) or Calvary (Latin). What does the word mean? (circle one)
    The Cemetery   The Place of Death
    The Place of the Skull The Killing Field

11. As soon as Jesus died, people all around Jerusalem started seeing resurrected saints.
    ___ Yes ___ No

12. What was done to speed up death during crucifixion? (circle one)
    Stabbing with a lance   Giving drugged wine
    Breaking legs   Strangulation

13. Who owned the tomb Jesus was placed in? (check one)
    ___ Nicodemus of Jerusalem
    ___ Lazarus of Bethany
    ___ Simon of Cyrene
    ___ Joseph of Arimathea

14. After the tomb was found to be empty, the soldiers who guarded it gave what excuse? (check one)
    ___ They were scared and ran away while guarding the tomb.
    ___ The disciples crept in and stole the body.
    ___ They got drunk and couldn't remember what happened.
    ___ Nothing. They couldn't be found.

15. For whom did Mary mistake the risen Lord? (circle one)
    An angel   A disciple   A gardener   A mourner

16. About how many people at one time saw Jesus alive after he was resurrected? (circle one)
    25   50   200   300   500   1,000

HOW TO USE
The Easter Quiz

Many kids (and adults as well) feel confident that they know the events that surround the crucifixion and resurrection of Christ. This questionnaire may surprise them by showing that they may not be as familiar with the details as they thought.

Suggested classroom activities

Use this questionnaire as a lead-in to the events of the Easter season. It can also be used as a contest or competition (guys against girls, juniors against seniors, or kids against parents).

Write the main events of the arrest, trial, crucifixion, and resurrection of Jesus on index cards, one event per card. Challenge your students to put them in chronological order without referring to the Bible. Make several sets of cards so small groups can compete. Even experts have trouble with this one!

Thinking through the questions

Question 1: The Passover (Matthew 26:18)

Question 2: Thirty pieces of silver (Matthew 26:15)

Question 3: Judas attempted to give the blood money back to the priests, but when they refused he scattered it on the floor of the temple (Matthew 27:5).

Question 4: No. Jesus was arrested by an armed group sent by the chief priests (see Matthew 26:47). Soldiers were present (John 18:3), probably as observers. They do not appear to have made the arrest itself.

Question 5: Jesus was beaten by both Roman and Jewish guards (Mark 14:63-65, 15:16-20).

Question 6: Pilate's wife advised him against dealing with Jesus based on a dream (Matthew 27:19).

Question 7: Yes. They gave homage in jest and mocking (Mark 15:17-20).

Question 8: Barabbas was the name of the prisoner (Mark 15:7).

Question 9: Simon, a foreigner from Cyrene, was drafted to carry the cross (Mark 15:21).

Question 10: The death site was called "The Place of the Skull" (Mark 15:22).

Question 11: True. This odd event is recorded in Matthew 27:52-53.

Question 12: Breaking of the legs was the method generally used to hurry death (John 19:31-33).

Question 13: Jesus was buried in the tomb belonging to Joseph of Arimathea (Luke 23:50).

Question 14: The guards were given money to say that the disciples had stolen the body while they slept (Matthew 28:11-15).

Question 15: Mary thought Jesus was a gardener (John 20:15-16).

Question 16: Over 500 people saw the resurrected Christ at the same time (1 Corinthians 15:6).

The Christmas IQ Test

1. As long as Christmas has been celebrated, it has been on December 25.
   ___ Yes ___ No

2. Joseph was from what area? (circle one)
   Bethlehem   Jerusalem   Cana   Egypt
   Minnesota   None of the above

3. How did Mary and Joseph travel to Bethlehem? (check one)
   ___ Camel   ___ Volkswagen
   ___ Donkey   ___ Joseph walked, Mary rode a donkey
   ___ Walked   ___ Who knows?

4. Mary and Joseph were married when Mary became pregnant.
   ___ Yes ___ No

5. Mary and Joseph were married when Jesus was born.
   ___ Yes ___ No

6. Mary was a virgin when she gave birth to Jesus.
   ___ Yes ___ No

7. What is a manger? (check one)
   ___ Stable for domestic animals ___ Feeding trough
   ___ Wooden hay storage bin   ___ Barn

8. What animals does the Bible say were present at Jesus' birth? (check one)
   ___ Cows, sheep, goats   ___ Lions, tigers, and bears
   ___ Cows, donkeys, sheep   ___ None of the above
   ___ Sheep and goats only

9. Who saw the star in the east? (check one)
   ___ Shepherds
   ___ Mary and Joseph
   ___ Three kings
   ___ The shepherds and the kings
   ___ None of the above

10. What sign did the angels tell the shepherds to look for? (check one)
    ___ This way to baby Jesus
    ___ A house with a Christmas tree
    ___ A star over Bethlehem
    ___ A baby in a manger
    ___ A baby that doesn't cry
    ___ None of the above

11. Where was there snow that first Christmas? (check one)
    ___ Only in Bethlehem   ___ Somewhere in Israel
    ___ All over Israel   ___ Nowhere in Israel
    ___ Mary and Joseph only dreamed of a white Christmas

12. What is frankincense? (check one)
    ___ A precious metal   ___ A precious perfume
    ___ A precious fabric   ___ An Eastern monster story

13. The wise men found Jesus in a what? (check one)
    ___ Manger ___ Stable ___ House ___ Holiday Inn

14. Why did the wise men stop in Jerusalem? (check one)
    ___ To inform Herod about Jesus
    ___ To find out where Jesus was
    ___ To ask about the star they saw
    ___ For gas
    ___ To buy presents for Jesus

15. Where do we find the Christmas story in order to check up on all these ridiculous questions? (check one)
    ___ (A)Matthew   ___ Only A and B
    ___ (B)Mark   ___ Only A and C
    ___ (C)Luke   ___ Only A, B, and C
    ___ (D)John   ___ Only X, Y, and Z
    ___ All of the above

16. How did you like this test? (circle one)
    Super   Great   Fantastic   All of the above

HOW TO USE
The Christmas IQ Test

Many kids (and adults as well) think they know a lot about Christmas. This test can be revealing, informative, and even embarrassing.

Suggested classroom activities

Use this questionnaire to lead into the events of the Christmas season. It can be used for an opener to a Bible study or as a contest or competition (guys against girls, juniors against seniors, or kids against parents).

Put the main events leading up to and including the birth of Christ on index cards, one event per card. Challenge your students to put them in chronological order without referring to the Bible. Make several sets of cards so small groups can compete after completing the questionnaire.

Thinking through the questions

Question 1: No. Not until the fourth century did it settle on December 25. Other dates were accepted before then.

Question 2: Bethlehem (Luke 2:3-4)

Question 3: Who knows? (the Bible doesn't say)

Question 4: No (Matthew 1:18)

Question 5: No (Luke 2:5)

Question 6: Yes (Matthew 1:25)

Question 7: Feeding trough.

Question 8: None of the above (the Bible doesn't specify)

Question 9: None of the above (the wise men—not kings did) (Matthew 2:1-2)

Question 10: A baby in a manger (Luke 2:12)

Question 11: Somewhere in Israel (Mt. Hermon is snow covered)

Question 12: Perfume

Question 13: In a house (Matthew 2:11)

Question 14: To find out where Jesus was (Matthew 2:1-2)

Question 15: Only A and C.

Question 16: All of the above (of course!).

Senior Survey

PLEASE PRINT!

Name _____ Age _____

Male ___ Female ___

Address _____

City _____ Zip_____

Phone _____ Date of Birth_____

1. Do you plan to go to a college or trade school this fall?
___ Yes ___ No
If yes, which one?

2. Do you have any kind of career in mind at this point?
___ Yes ___ No
If yes, what is it?

If you are not planning to go to college or trade school, please go to Question 7.

3. Is the school you want to attend a Christian college?
___ Yes ___ No

4. Are you familiar with Christian organizations which might be active on your prospective campus?
___ Yes ___ No ___ No, but I would like to find out

5. Where do you plan to live? (check one)
___ School dormitory ___ With relatives
___ Off campus ___ At home

6. Will you be moving out of the area to attend school?
___ Yes ___ No

7. Do you have any job lined up after you graduate?
___ Yes ___ No
If yes, what is it?

8. How do you feel about graduating from high school? (check all that apply)
___ Excited ___ Anxious
___ Scared ___ Pressured
___ Sad ___ Depressed
___ Relieved ___ Numb
___ Ho-hum

9. What would you say were the most meaningful things you learned or experienced as a part of our high school group?

10. Who made a positive difference in your life during your high school years?

11. If you could live your high school years over again, what would you do differently?

12. Which of the following, if any, do you feel you have not been adequately trained to do? (check those that apply)
___ Balance checkbook ___ Write reports
___ Figure taxes ___ Do math problems
___ Wash clothes ___ Use correct grammar
___ Cook ___ Spell
___ Clean ___ Write résumés
___ Other:

HOW TO USE
Senior Survey

This questionnaire is an ideal tool to use with your high school seniors. Who will be moving on? Where are they going? Who is staying around?

Suggested classroom activities

Senior Survey can give you an idea of how the church might be able to help prepare or inform these young men and women.

For example, if your seniors do not feel that high school has prepared them to do simple tasks such as balancing a checkbook or figuring elementary taxes, it may be appropriate to have someone with the proper skills conduct a special training session for seniors only.

If your students need information about Christian colleges, provide that data.

This questionnaire can be a perfect lead-in to using Laurie Polich's four-session preparation course *Facing Your Future*, published by Youth Specialties. It's designed to prepare seniors for life after youth group. To order, call 1-800-776-8008.

Thinking through the questions

Most of the questions center primarily around your students' plans. The answers will tell you who will remain available to serve as leaders or sponsors and who may return with new skills.

Other questions, particularly from question 8 on, deal with student's opinions and experiences during the youth group years. Use this information to tighten up your future plans.

The Crazy Christmas Quiz

1. What do bad kids get in their stockings?

2. Name all nine of Santa's Reindeer:

    1.   6.

    2.   7.

    3.   8.

    4.   9.

    5.

3. What is the name of the horse that pulls the sleigh in the song *Jingle Bells?*

4. The English call Santa Claus by what name?

5. What was the name of the first ghost to visit Scrooge in Charles Dickens' *A Christmas Carol?*

6. What was the weather like on Rudolph the Red-Nosed Reindeer's maiden voyage?

7. Who is the mythical creature that "nips at your nose" during the Christmas season?

8. According to the poem *The Night Before Christmas*, what kind of dancing apparitions appeared in the dreams of the children on Christmas Eve?

9. The kids lead Frosty the Snowman down the streets of town to whom?

10. What do we deck the halls with?

11. What parasitical vegetation can cause people to pucker?

12. Who is the person credited with first putting lights (in this case, candles) on a Christmas tree?

13. In the movie *A Christmas Story*, a school boy dreamed and wished for what toy?

14. Who stole Christmas?

15. In the classic Christmas movie *It's a Wonderful Life*, what happened every time a bell rang?

HOW TO USE
The Crazy Christmas Quiz

This is a simple Christmas trivia test that makes a light-hearted game or crowd breaker.

Suggested classroom activities
The best time for this questionnaire is during the Christmas season. You'll find many cool ideas for a Christmas party in *Holiday Ideas for Youth Groups: Revised Edition* (Wayne Rice and Mike Yaconelli, Youth Specialties). To order, call 1-800-776-8008.

Thinking through the questions
The answers to the questions are given below, just in case you didn't quite get every one.
Question 1: Coal
Question 2: Comet, Cupid, Donner, Blitzen, Dasher, Dancer, Prancer, Vixen, and Rudolph
Question 3: Bobtail
Question 4: Father Christmas
Question 5: Jacob Marley
Question 6: Foggy
Question 7: Jack Frost
Question 8: Sugar plums
Question 9: A traffic cop
Question 10: Boughs of holly
Question 11: Mistletoe
Question 12: Martin Luther
Question 13: A Red Ryder BB Gun
Question 14: The Grinch
Question 15: An angel received its wings

See if you can figure out which common Christmas saying is being presented in each "translation." (The first is answered as an example.)

1. Move hitherward the entire assembly of those who are loyal in their belief
   Answer: O Come, All Ye Faithful

2. Listen, the celestial messengers produce harmonious sounds
   Answer:

3. Nocturnal time span of unbroken quietness
   Answer:

4. An emotion excited by the acquisition or expectation of good given to the terrestrial sphere
   Answer:

5. Embellish the interior passageways
   Answer:

6. Twelve o'clock midnight on a clement night witnessed its arrival
   Answer:

7. The Christmas preceding all others
   Answer:

8. Diminutive masculine master of skin-covered percussionistic cylinders
   Answer:

9. Omnipotent supreme being who elicits respite to ecstatic distinguished males
   Answer:

10. Expectation of arrival to populated area by mythical, masculine perennial gift-giver
    Answer:

11. Natal celebration devoid of color
    Answer:

12. Geographic state of fantasy during the season of mother nature's dormancy
    Answer:

13. The first person nominative plural of a triumvirate of far Eastern heads of state
    Answer:

14. Tintinnabulation of vacillating pendulums in inverted, metallic, resonant cups
    Answer:

15. In a distant location the existence of an improvised unit of newborn children's slumber furniture
    Answer:

HOW TO USE
Christmas Synonyms

This is a great way to break the ice during any Christmas party. It can be used with all age groups, but high school kids and older will have an easier time figuring out some of the terms.

Suggested classroom activities

Small groups can be assigned five phrases each to translate. The first group to finish correctly wins.

You'll find many cool ideas for a Christmas party in *Holiday Ideas for Youth Groups: Revised Edition* (Wayne Rice and Mike Yaconelli, Youth Specialties). To order, call 1-800-776-8008.

Thinking through the questions

Were you able to get them all? If not, here are the answers.

Question 1: O Come, All Ye Faithful

Question 2: Hark, the Herald Angels Sing

Question 3: Silent Night

Question 4: Joy to the World

Question 5: Deck the Halls

Question 6: It Came Upon a Midnight Clear

Question 7: The First Noel

Question 8: Little Drummer Boy

Question 9: God Rest Ye Merry Gentlemen

Question 10: Santa Claus Is Coming to Town

Question 11: White Christmas

Question 12: Winter Wonderland

Question 13: We Three Kings of Orient Are

Question 14: Jingle Bells

Question 15: Away in a Manger

Cartoon Trivia Test

1. What kind of baby bird is always trying to get Foghorn Leghorn, the rooster?

2. Name Donald Duck's nephews.

    1.   2.   3.

3. What is the name of the lovesick skunk of Warner Brothers fame?

4. What is the name of Roger Rabbit's wife?

5. Name the seven dwarfs from Disney's *Snow White and the Seven Dwarfs*.

    1.   5.

    2.   6.

    3.   7.

    4.

6. Name the friendly ghost.

7. What is the name of the hungry character who is always trying to catch the Roadrunner?

8. What is the name of Fred Flintstone's daughter?

9. What is the name of the wise-cracking bird in Disney's *Aladdin*?

10. What is the name of the orchid-eating dog in the old *Popeye* cartoons?

11. What did the Beast give to Belle so that she could remember him?

12. What does Calvin's dad (in the comic strip *Calvin and Hobbes*) do for work?

13. What cartoon character starred in the first cartoon made with sound?

14. What is the name given to virtually all products and companies in Warner Brothers' cartoons?

15. Alice the Goon was in love with what cartoon figure?

16. Who is the photographer that works at the Daily Planet alongside Lois Lane and Clark Kent?

17. Charles Schultz is the creator of which popular comic strip?

18. Walt Disney's *Cinderella* featured a mean cat by what name?

19. Who is Yogi Bear's sidekick?

20. What is Porky Pig's famous closing line?

HOW TO USE
Cartoon Trivia Test

This questionnaire makes a great icebreaker. Most teenagers have a long and varied history of watching cartoons and reading the comic pages, so a quiz on this subject gives kids a chance to dredge their memories for answers.

Suggested classroom activities

Use as a pencil-and-paper test, or simply read the questions and award small prizes (like comics and cartoon videos) to the first person to stand with the right answer for each question.

This questionnaire can be used during a video evening where cartoons will be shown or during a game night based on or suggested by cartoon characters (for example, Coyote versus Roadrunner relay race).

Thinking through the questions

Question 1: Henry, a baby chicken hawk

Question 2: Huey, Dewey, and Louie

Question 3: Pepe Le Pew

Question 4: Jessica Rabbit

Question 5: Doc, Sneezy, Grumpy, Sleepy, Bashful, Happy, and Dopey

Question 6: Casper

Question 7: Wile E. Coyote

Question 8: Pebbles

Question 9: Yago

Question 10: The Jeep

Question 11: A mirror

Question 12: He's a lawyer

Question 13: Mickey Mouse

Question 14: ACME

Question 15: Popeye

Question 16: Jimmy Olson

Question 17: Peanuts

Question 18: Lucifer

Question 19: Boo-Boo

Question 20: Th-th-th-that's all, folks!

What's Your IQ?

1. You are in a rectangular house where all the windows face south. As you look out the window, a bear walks by. What color is the bear?

2. A plane crash occurred on the USA/Canadian border. In which country did they bury the survivors?

3. Does England have a Fourth of July?

4. If you had a match and entered a room in which there were a kerosene lamp, an oil heater, and a wood-burning stove, which would you light first?

5. If you went to bed at 8:00 a.m. and set the alarm clock to get up at 9 o'clock the next morning how many hours of sleep would you get?

6. Some months have thirty days, some have thirty-one days. How many have twenty-eight days?

7. How far can a dog run into the woods?

8. What four words appear on every denomination of U.S. coin?

9. What is the minimum number of baseball players on the field during any part of an inning in a regular game?

   How many outs per inning?

10. A person is holding two U.S. coins which total fifty-five cents in value. One is not a nickel. What are the two coins?

11. A farmer bought seventeen sheep; all but nine died. How many does he have left?

12. Divide thirty by one-half and add ten. What is the answer?

13. Take two apples from three apples and what do you have?

14. An archaeologist claimed he found some gold coins dated 46 B.C. How do you know his claim is not true?

15. A woman gives a beggar fifty cents. The woman is the beggar's sister but the beggar is not the woman's brother. Why not?

16. How many animals of each species did Moses take aboard the ark with him?

17. Where was Paul going on the road to Damascus?

18. A drunk plowed his car into another vehicle that had a driver and a passenger. The drunk and the driver were not injured, but the passenger was pulled out dead. The drunk was not charged with manslaughter. Why?

19. What word in this test is mispelled?

20. Why isn't it legal in North Carolina for a man to marry his widow's sister?

HOW TO USE
What's Your IQ?

This is one of those silly questionnaires that can be used during a party as an event opener, icebreaker, or contest.

Suggested classroom activities
Set a short time limit for the test so that kids are forced to rush through the test. (Three minutes is usually good enough.) Have the kids place their tests face down until the signal to begin is given. Read the answers at the end of the time period and wait for the groans to begin.

If you really want to get silly, buy or borrow some toys that test your intelligence (such as the baby toys that have plastic shapes that go through matching holes) and time teams for speed.

Thinking through the questions
Question 1: White (you are at the North Pole)
Question 2: You don't bury survivors
Question 3: Yes
Question 4: The match
Question 5: One hour
Question 6: Twelve
Question 7: Halfway (After that, it is running out of the woods)
Question 8: "United States of America" or "In God We Trust"
Question 9: Ten (nine fielders and a batter); six outs per inning
Question 10: A fifty cent piece and a nickel (one is not a nickel but the other is)
Question 11: Nine
Question 12: Seventy (thirty divided *in* half is 15, but divided *by* one-half it's 60)
Question 13: Two
Question 14: The B.C. dating system did not exist until after Christ was born
Question 15: They are sisters
Question 16: None (Noah took the animals, not Moses)
Question 17: Damascus
Question 18: The passenger was dead before the accident (the other car in the accident was a hearse)
Question 19: Mispelled (misspelled is the correct sppellling)
Question 20: He's already dead.

A Walk in the Woods

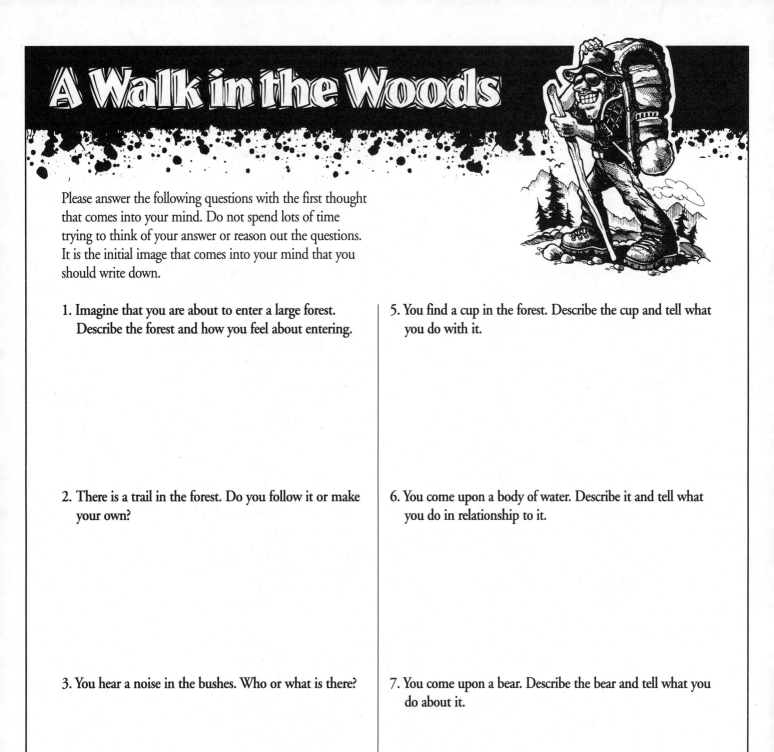

Please answer the following questions with the first thought that comes into your mind. Do not spend lots of time trying to think of your answer or reason out the questions. It is the initial image that comes into your mind that you should write down.

1. Imagine that you are about to enter a large forest. Describe the forest and how you feel about entering.

2. There is a trail in the forest. Do you follow it or make your own?

3. You hear a noise in the bushes. Who or what is there?

4. You find a key in the forest. Describe the key and tell what you do with it.

5. You find a cup in the forest. Describe the cup and tell what you do with it.

6. You come upon a body of water. Describe it and tell what you do in relationship to it.

7. You come upon a bear. Describe the bear and tell what you do about it.

8. You come upon a wall. Describe the wall and tell what you do in relationship to it.

HOW TO USE
A Walk in the Woods

Y ou can tell the kids that this is a test to deeply probe their inner psyches, but in reality it's just meaningless silliness.

Suggested classroom activities

A Walk in the Woods is best used with a smaller group and at a quiet event such as a home party.

You can have the whole group take this test, or ask for three or four volunteers to take the test and then read their results. It is important that no one talks about what they have written until all have completed the test.

Alternatively, kids could respond verbally to each question. In this case, other volunteers should wait out of earshot.

Thinking through the questions

There is symbolism in each question.

Question 1: The Forest. This describes your outlook on life. A dark mysterious forest means that life is a deep mystery for you. A scary, spooky forest means you are fearful of life. If the forest is bright and cheerful, your outlook is positive. If your forest is on fire, it means you are a psycho.

Question 2: The Trail. If you follow the existing trail, you tend to follow rules. Making your own trail means that you are independent or too cool to follow guidelines.

Question 3: The Noise. The noise in the bushes symbolizes the unknown. For some it will remain a mystery, for others there will be satisfactory answers.

Question 4: The Key. This symbolizes education. Some will keep their key, some will toss it away or ignore it. Others may describe a beautiful key, a functional key, or a pile of rust.

Question 5: The Cup. This symbolizes religion. Some find a chalice, others a Styrofoam cup.

Question 6: The Water. The body of water speaks of romance. Some find a huge lake and want to skinny dip, other find a dank swamp and want to avoid it at all costs.

Question 7: The Bear. Here we have problems or troubles. Some will see a scary bear and run from their troubles. Some will see a harmless cub and pet it.

Question 8: The Wall. Death is symbolized by the wall. Some will turn around at the wall. Some will crawl over. Some will see it as a barbed-wire fence, some as a picket fence or crumbling rock pile. Some fear death or want to avoid it, others approach with confidence.

THE DATA COMPLIANCE TEST

Instructions: Please answer each question in sequence. Read through the entire test before starting on the first question.

1. Print your name in the upper right hand corner of the test.

2. Find the word that is not spelled right in this sentance and circle it.

3. Draw a triangle in the bottom left corner of this paper.

4. Uganda is found on which continent? (circle one)
   Asia   Africa   North America   Europe   Australia

5. With your pen or pencil darken in every "o" found in this sentence and the ones in the question above.

6. Raise your hand and do not put it down until you are recognized.

7. Draw a circle in the middle of the triangle you have already drawn.

8. In cursive, put your name on the top left corner of this paper.

9. What is the sum of 4+8+3-9?

Write the answer here: _____

10. Tear off the bottom right corner of this paper.

11. Find all of the words in this question and in the above sentence that have the letter "f" in them and put a square around them. Then count how many you have found and place the total here: _____

12. Put your age in the bottom middle of the paper.

13. Stand up and say, "I have reached this point."

14. Put an outline of your hand on the back of this test.

15. Put a line through the title of this test.

16. Crow like a rooster loud enough so everyone can hear you.

17. Underline any word in this sentence or the one above that starts with the same letter as your first name.

18. Hold your breath and count to forty.

19. Count how many words are in this sentence and put the number here: _____

20. Ignore all of the questions on this test except the first one. Just print your name and wait quietly until the time is up.

The Data Compliance Test

This is a very fun questionnaire with a gimmick—read the last question on the quiz to see what it is. The purpose of this questionnaire is to teach the importance of following instructions.

Suggested classroom activities

You can crank up the anticipation and the likelihood that kids will rush into the questionnaire by promising a prize for those who finish it completely and properly within a given amount of time.

When the kids finish (and realize they've been stung), you can talk about the importance of following instructions carefully—especially the instructions for living found in the Bible.

Thinking through the questions

The correct way to do this quiz is to read and obey the instructions before starting. Everyone who does this will see that all students have to do is write their names on the paper and wait until the time is up.